LET'S GO FOR A WALK
by
JONATHAN SEAN CHERLIN

Oded Halahmy Foundation for the Arts, Inc.
Special Edition

LET'S GO FOR A WALK

Cover Design & Photography by Three Headed Vision

Taken on site at Walter M's mural; Teddy White Pl. and 31st Ave., Queens

Models- Front: Cal Cerberus; Back: Jonathan Cherlin, Jazireh the Dachshund

Copyright © 2015 Jonathan Sean Cherlin

All rights reserved.

LET'S GO FOR A WALK

DEDICATION

To Alexis,
A promise is a promise.

To Grandpa,
I will try to remember that I am
"...smarter than I think I am..."

To Grandma,
I make sure, as you instructed, that I
"Laugh everyday".

To Dad,
Thanks for all the
improvised bed-time stories.

To Mom,
Thanks for always telling me to,
"Use your words."

To my Sister,
My first short-story was dedicated to you
in Second Grade.
So, my first book should be as well.
At least I spelled "Sister" correctly this time.

To all my Friends and Family,
Thank you for supporting me
in everything that I seek to accomplish.
You are all my comfort and inspiration.

LET'S GO FOR A WALK

CONTENTS

Acknowledgments	i
Foreword	ii
Waiting to Be Found	1
2012	2
2013	27
2014	88
2015	142

ACKNOWLEDGMENTS

Thank you Michael Geffner, Megan DiBello, and The Oded Halahmy Foundation for making this possible. Thank you, Cal Cerberus for being my friend and for doing my cover art...You have always been a prime source of creativity and inspiration. Thanks to all my fellow Inspired Word creators.

FOREWORD

The enclosed work is both Fiction and Non-Fiction, since I sometimes find Fiction to be more True than actual events. Therefore, if you believe that one of my poems might be about you then you are probably correct and false at the same time. The format will detail my mental and emotional state from 2012 through 2015. It is a story of self-reflection, loneliness, and getting over a girl. As you read, I advise that you envision us walking down a dimly lit city street at midnight...since that is the environment in which these thoughts, feelings, and stories are best discussed. So, let's go for a walk...

LET'S GO FOR A WALK

The following is the only poem I have memorized. I wrote it when I was 16-years-old. I find that it still applies to my life at the age of 31.

WAITING TO BE FOUND

I walk down a path

Lost, I leave my light on to be found

As I walk I see other lights

I try to get to them

Some turn their lights out before they can be found

Some I meet with and we walk together side by side

Until we walk our separate ways

Not knowing if we'll meet in future days

Infinite paths lie ahead

Some going back, some going forward

But I never wish to go back

Because there are demons there

Demons who will tear you apart until you are dead

And I know that my destiny lies somewhere ahead

Again and again I realize I walk alone

But I will forever leave my light on and hope I'll be discovered

Finally found by someone who will walk with me

'Til the end of this long dark forest is uncovered

LET'S GO FOR A WALK

2012

LET'S GO FOR A WALK

The Theme is Truth
(09/08/2012)

Honesty of all things is the purest form of deception.
It is something that many of us try to attain,
but as soon as words leave our synapses
they turn to lies.
Honesty, would be to keep quiet.
True truth is when we don't speak,
when we let the emotion and thought wash over us, zap through our brain
canals, and maybe even move our tongue but never vibrate our gullet.
I've heard many speak the false truths,
"I love you", "I'll be there for you", "I'll be hanging out with a 'friend'"
but half-truths are no truths
true honesty is full and cannot be divided into equal parts.

So what the fuck man?
You say that you're interested in someone, and you never tell that it's
someone you shouldn't be interested in?
What the fuck man?
You know better, but you continue the affair
you continue the lies and you continue to not see the difference between
conflict and just deception.

We're in a post-modern-apocalyptic time.
Where society seized to exist because people were no longer required to
make sense.

We walk down a single road.
I've seen it before.
It's grimy and smells like coffee and shit.
We stop at a local bar.
The scent turns to beer, and the noise is a cacophony of laughter and
sorrow.
I instantly spot 5 girls I'd like to fuck, and go over to the bar, and order a
Bud.

LET'S GO FOR A WALK

"That's five...", says the bartender...I hand him a $20, he breaks it...I give him a two-dollar-tip and walk through the crowd.
I know that if someone really looked, they would spot who didn't belong like a Where's Waldo picture.
"I never know where to stand" I think,
when the truth is
that I never know where to stand where I could blend.

And movies can be a good escape if they mirror the internal struggle because once again,
the only true self-conflicts are the ones unspoken.
But movies, are nothing but someone elses' feelings
flickering through shades of colors pixel to pixel moving along as if they really want to exist that bad.
A video game is only this, except I move the pixels.
A dream is a pixel-less video game.
A dream is the closest thing to me playing me.
I am a pixel-less video game.

If I were to hunt, it would be an imaginary animal inside of my brain
and the game would ultimately end up being me
because I am everything in my dreams
unless it's true that dreams exist when we're awake
and if that's the case
then there really is no difference at all between this world and that
so I might as well be dreaming there when I'm awake.

When did it last happen that I fell for someone?
Well I'd say about 5 years ago,
and before that, I'd say 3 years,
and before that I'd say, 2 years,
and before that I'd say 1,
and before that , 8 months,
and before that 5 months,
and before that 3 months,
and before that 2 months,
and before that 1 month,

LET'S GO FOR A WALK

before that 1 week,
before that 5 days,
before that 3,
before that 2,
before that 1,
and when I was a child I'd fall for someone new every passing hour,
minute, second...

But now that buzzing in my ear won't quit,
my body clenches,
and my heart skips beat after beat
and I wonder when it will stop.

Ya see, I've always known that I will die young
I don't know how or when it will happen
I don't know how or why I know
But it's soon.

The day will come soon when I won't exist anywhere
the day will come soon when I'll really no longer be able to speak at all
I feel the Earth rejecting me as an immune system fights a germ
except this disease won't spread,
and I have already been isolated from the rest of the body.
It's only a matter of time when someone says,
"There once was something like a man here
he is gone now
he was here once before
and you won't see him, hear him, feel him,
if that was anything you ever really did to begin with".

But the words go onwards and outwards,
and I can't contain the lies I need to tell anymore
the truth is that the lies are my only way to the truth
fore how can you ever understand something
without exploring its opposite.

LET'S GO FOR A WALK

True story
A man stood on the subway today.
An old man stood on the subway today.
A homeless man stood on the subway today,
holding out his elongated brown/black/blue fingernails
staring at them in awe.
I stared as well repulsed, and amazed
there is beauty in this man.
But we can't touch him,
we can't help him,
and we'd rather he didn't ruin our morning coffee.

It's been a long time since I've been a we.
People think I'm one of them,
or one of many,
or people don't really think at all.
The truth is I am
the truth is to think.
The truth is that no one's ever blamed you for lying in your sleep.

And they laugh out there,
and they scream out there,
and they die out there,
and they dream out there,
and I can somehow see it,
I somehow know them,
I'm the muse,
I'm the wind,
I'm the nothingness,
the coldness that slips through your pours like liquid nitrogen,
stiffening your muscles and lulling you to rest
no motion can resist my arrest.

And there are those that have loved me,
and those that I've loved.
But now I'm surrounded by dust.
The sky still shines when I sleep.

LET'S GO FOR A WALK

The moon still watches where I once strolled on the side of a highway
with my best friend in the car driving beside me,
knowing that I needed to run and see and roll around for awhile
But he's not here now either
so why am I?

The truth is that nothing really matters.
The truth is that which is silent.
The truth is...

Thoughts in The Realm of Potential
(09/16/2012)

There are alternate worlds that we call Thoughts.
A Thought might be a universe unto itself,
filled with characters, places, things
that are quite familiar yet effected by
a filter of our own imaginings.
Some think that Thoughts can predict the future.
But I think that Thoughts produce the future.
It is said that the average human being
has about 70,000 Thoughts per day.
With about 7 billion people on Earth,
that would be 490 trillion alternate universes per day.
Alternate universes where ideas and happenings take place
that may never reach the light of reality.

However, there are many Thoughts
that do crossover into our plane of existence
Their spaceship has a name
it's called "Action".
Action is the only way a Thought can travel
into reality.

So, there it is.
Thoughts become reality
with Action.
And, as soon as something becomes reality,
it in turn effects what is already real
which in turn were Thoughts that became reality,
and effected what is real
and so on and so forth.

LET'S GO FOR A WALK

So, every Thought put into Action
effects every other Thought that's been put into Action
travelling through space and time together.

But then what of the Thoughts contained in the void?
What of the Thoughts that remain in the planes of
"What if?" or
"What could have been?" in the realm of
"Potential"
They have the contradictory effect.
They implode reality
they suck away what could have happened
and have an effect by nullification
decreasing the possibilities of our real universe.

I wonder how many realities there are of just words
I wonder how many verses of famous poems never made it here.
I wonder how many amazing characters have never travelled
how many stories never even put to paper
how many notes never heard
images never visualized
sensations never materialized.

How many are evil?
How many are good?
Can a Thought be good or evil?
Or are they like children,
and were just brought up that way?

And what of the Thoughts that are raised by others?
When a man or woman pays for the Action
of another to accompany the Thought to conception
does it become bastardized?

LET'S GO FOR A WALK

Is it unnatural?
Or, is it then a hybrid of two
or more Thoughts becoming one?

They say that an Idea is indestructible
immortal
that no matter how many times you think you've killed it,
it'll eventually pop up again and again in different places.
But why?
It's almost as if that every time Action
is about to speed forth,
every Thought wants to get on board
and what's stopping them is Conscience and Fear
sometimes guards tire though,
and let a couple through that weren't ever intended to come to Action.
Mistakes
mistakes that may cause regret or redemption.
Fore an unintended Thought
is a loose cannon
a Wild Card set to random.

However, what's even more terrifying,
is that Action is a ship that goes both ways.
That what really happened can become just a Thought,
through History being erased from Reality.

Therefore, Reality is not nearly as static as most think.
That Thought and Reality
flow forth and fro from
"What If",
"What could have been", and
"What might have happened" freely.

LET'S GO FOR A WALK

So, next time you think,
I advise you to keep track of where it is going.
Is Action's destination Reality,
or is it a return trip?
Have you let a fugitive on board?
Is it dangerous or benevolent?
Either way, without Action
we are all just Thoughts
in the endless realm of Potential.

LET'S GO FOR A WALK
09/23/2012

It is the job of those who know where they're going,
to look out for those who seem lost.

On a path, looking for a guide
I feel anguished and tired,
angry and abused.
The absurdity of this world has led me astray
and I keep searching for a way to live,
a way to breathe freely,
a way to allow myself the comforts of intimacy.
But I can't stay here.
I always seem to be out the door.
I can't breathe here.
I can't see where this is taking me
and I'm afraid and need you.
I ache for the warmth of those arms
that enraptured me in love and kindness.
I die each day that I can't call you,
can't see your deep blue saviors of sea.
Those eyes that reached into my soul,
were also the very things that plucked it out of me.
And to know that you still need me in your life,
and to know that you still think of me, still wonder about me,
that we're still telekinetically connected.
I'm tired of explaining myself.
These words won't do it either,
they won't do the trick of describing the only emotion
that I've been certain is Love.
This might be corny, melodramatic,
but I don't give a shit.

LET'S GO FOR A WALK

I need to forget you.
I need that machine from Eternal Sunshine
to make my mind Spotless.
I want you erased.
I want me back.
I want what you stole from me, and freely give to others.

It's funny how you can't really guzzle something from a wine glass.
That it's designed to be sipped upon.
It's designed to let the drug slowly drip into your blood stream
until you're intoxicated.

My mind strays from the point,
although I'm not quite sure there was one to begin with.
Something about being lost.
Something about living like an Alley Cat,
rummaging through garbage,
suffering through his freedom and independence.

It is the job of those who know where they're going,
to look out for those who seem lost.

This is something I keep telling myself.
This is something that I've always done
for others
back when I knew where I was going.
However, few are willing to lend a helping hand
to nudge in the right direction.

Most get angry and instruct
to "Figure it out on your own!!"
But that's not fair.
Just because you did,

LET'S GO FOR A WALK

doesn't mean I can.
I am completely lost and vulnerable.
The idea of gaining my footing,
and remembering where to go,
seems like a dream.
There's nothing here.
Nothing to hold onto, nothing to love, nothing to hate,
nothing to care about now that Rachel is gone.
And I cringe at your name.
Rachel.
And I want to ask again and again for you to Love me more than a friend.
Again and again, year after year, I suffered the No.
I suffered your No. Now you must continue to suffer mine.

It is the job of those who know where they're going,
to look out for those who seem lost.

So I walk down this street.
Turning left and right and left and right.
I see a pedestrian and ask for directions
but once they turn around
it's always you
it's always Rachel.
And so, I don't ask anymore
I prefer to be lost.

Madness
(11/10/2012)

I lie awake,
because sometimes we don't have time
for the subtlety of dreams.
Stuff sitting on my mind.
I recline
in a fantasy world of my own creating,
nibbling at the fact
that reality and illusion
teeter on the extraordinary.
And you can't save a life
that you don't possess in some form.
You can't save a life
because you can't take one.
You can only live a life,
or choose not to live one
although that is illegal.
So I'll continue.
I'll choose to go on.
I'll definitely not decide to take one.
I might at some point give one.
But again, that means ownership
and I don't know if I can handle that responsibility right now
not that anyone's currently asking me to.

But you, my Man,
live your life differently
it's all about the game,
and the winning, over losing,
and you HAVE to win you have to WIN the game

LET'S GO FOR A WALK

or you'll lose it,
and that's the way you see the game of Life
and you must win you can't not win,
and death is both at the forefront
and not on your mind at all
because in the end
we all lose.

So write it down and forget about it.
The only way to express this
is to NOT make sense,
and therefore let's continue the absurdity
of words that cannot communicate fact,
but only the taste of it.
The delirium of confusing arrays,
of Ophelia complexes,
and what is a song without the lyric that makes you hear something else
but still channel the meaning
the purer meaning
the most truthful
because it wasn't what the author intended
the one that makes you talk about it
for 30 years on a technology
that didn't exist back then.

I told you that I'm lost,
and you told me to step up or get out
But life doesn't work in blacks and whites,
and the truth is gray and pink and red all over
the truth is not form or notions
or competitions of contracts with citations
the truth is the white-space in between the forms

LET'S GO FOR A WALK

the truth is around the word gripping at it.

And again I'm talking about truth,
but you can't talk about truth
because it defeats the purpose.
So, let's unravel this mystery
of the meaning of love and life and illusion.
Let's get confused.
Let's ask unanswerable questions
to the people least likely to understand the question in the first place.
Let's laugh without being provoked
and cry when we're happy
because we're so happy we're so sad
that it's not going to last very long.

A 93-year-old man who was once a genius,
who was once a musician, an artist, a writer,
a communist, a politician, a psychologist,
and above all a teacher
now reduced to being carried up three steps to eat dinner
with a son who only travels to see him once a year
but this time vacations are cut short
this time the son is forced to realize that his father can no longer

walk on his own
urinate on his own
undress on his own.
And the 93-year-old man is forced
to no longer fully realize anything ever again.
But must lose his dignity
must lose his memory
and must give up his sanity

LET'S GO FOR A WALK

in public
in front of those he's loved the most.

But the joys of capitalism.
The Honor of America
where you are free to die in poverty.
Where you are free to be forced into debt,
so an old man can die at home
hopefully, soon.
Because, if you can't work then you're expendable.
And if you can't work for cheap then you're expendable.
And if you don't like that,
then you're dangerous
and have to be put down.

So I ask you, Sir,
what is the point of getting to work on time today.
What is the point of waking up, bathing, getting dressed
and making this trip here
when it'll never be good enough.
Where it just continues this nightmare of a disillusioned society
where I know how confused I am,
and am fully aware that I can't ask a question
without being reprimanded.
The world is madness.
The world is but a fantasy,
the world is a waking nightmare without comfort without stability.
But when I lie here
when I lie neither dreaming, not fully awake
when nothing makes sense I see the clarity
I see why we must all die
before we go insane.

LET'S GO FOR A WALK

__Sandy__
(11/10/2012)

There must be a reason that we enjoy harmonization so much.
Two or more people singing on different levels,
but sounding as one.
It represents unification in differences.
It calls out something instinctual in our pack animal DNA.
However, dissonance seems to overthrow unity.
It is something that, most of the time, is undesirable to listen to.
But in the daily actions we take, as a species,
we support dissonance over harmony.

So I drove home after visiting a friend for the weekend.
I heard that a hurricane would hit
but, like many others,
I didn't believe what the media said anymore.
I don't trust the politicians anymore.
And, I've lived long enough to understand that both
are being run by hype and money.
However, there was always that aching panic in my heart.
That thing that says, "Maybe I should still listen..."
that thing that says, don't take anything TOO lightly EVER.

So, just in case the media and politicians
were not lying to me,
I decided I wanted to drive home
My REAL home,
the home that my family lives in
Or at least my first family,
for on my travels I've acquired more than one, more than two

LET'S GO FOR A WALK

Sitting for an hour at the Throgs Neck Bridge,
because even though it's a "State of Emergency",
the city still wants your money
and you have to pay your toll.

When I get home
my mother's happy to see me.
I get the word
that my father's on his way,
and he's bringing my grandfather
because Long Beach is being evacuated.

I decide to take a shower,
while I wait for their arrival.
I think it's a little funny
that we're afraid of a hurricane
and I'm taking a shower
I guess water is not always JUST water.

I get dressed
and come down stairs
to greet my grandfather
whose dementia seems to be light today.
He's joking around,
and there are moments
loud echos
of the philosopher and teacher
he once was.
Moments such as him
looking at the large decorative wooden bowl
my mother has on the table in the den
He asks,

LET'S GO FOR A WALK

"What is the significance of an empty bowl?"
I look at him inquisitively
as he smiles and says,
"What was, was."
Brilliant.

The next day proves to be less pleasant.
I work from home,
until the power goes out.
The storm is hitting.
Later we hear on the radio
the terror that this coast is going through.
I hear my grandfather's city
Long Beach
the city that I lived in until I was 12
the city that has my grandparents' house,
my second home
the city that has my entire childhood,
much of my adolescence,
and many of my adulthood memories of
fun, fear, crying, safety, love
being washed away.

Days later,
I hitch a ride back to Astoria,
since I'm told work is important,
and being a coder,
as long as I have power
I have work.
I hear of people homeless, hungry, without water,
without power, no one's helping them
this was my town

LET'S GO FOR A WALK

this was where I lived

I hear of Far Rockaway,
another town swept by water
I speak to my best friend
who freely admits that if she hadn't been
in New Orleans (of all places) for the last two weeks
she wouldn't have evacuated.

She comes home to a wasteland.
I have her stay with me for a weekend.
All her possessions,
all her things,
all her hopes,
all her memories
that she worked so hard for
without a family to help
all on her own
swept by the current
of an angry world
that we refuse to take care of.

Bloomberg wants the marathon to continue.
The people in charge,
bring the business areas
and the rich areas
back to life
because the rat race
must go on.

While those who already had next to nothing,
now have more nothing than they've ever NOT had.
And they're isolated.

LET'S GO FOR A WALK

And the media says it's old news.
And I go back to the office,
in Cooper Square,
where the rich people talk
about how happy they are to be back
because they were getting so sad
stuck in their warm heated apartments.

Dissonance is all around us now.
We are so broken.

The snow falls
and the rich dream of the close by holidays,
the winter wonderlands,
sing songs.

While the snow falls,
and the poor
the middle class
the 'unlucky'
moan, and mourn
the gurgling cries of their loved ones drowning.

The dissonance the waves bring,
washing away the grit,
only harmonizing in the depths of the ocean.

LET'S GO FOR A WALK
12/02/2012

Harmony.
An off-beat drum.
Is all I ask for.
The cold eyes of doubt.
The desire to end the classification
of a world that asks for persecution.
Wants me to judge and be judged.
That was not on Maslow's hierarchy of needs.
The realization
that if you really want Time to stop,
then it will.
Easily locking myself
in my room,
nothing happens here
When I'm only connected to the world
through flickering lights on a screen,
I feel safe in my cage.
Hamlet says,
"...Denmark is a prison."
Rosencrantz says,
"Why then your ambition makes it one.
'Tis too narrow for your mind."
And isn't that the case,
locked away in my thoughts.
No matter where I go,
I'm never free.
The shackles of a life
pining after someone I can't have.
My prime desire to never be satisfied,

LET'S GO FOR A WALK

leaving all other desires seemingly meaningless.
Too angry,
and this sounds absolutely ridiculous in my head.
The sadness seems infinitely similar to an excuse to not live my life.
Always running from the true problems of self-doubt
and I can't go about blaming anyone for it anymore.
I'm aware that I'm completely in control at this point,
but too stubborn
too furious at what I've thought Destiny was unfair about.
So, I'm defying Destiny
I'm refusing to follow my path, any path.
And instead sit in my sweat
and think of all the things I want,
that I refuse to pursue in the name
of my personal war against Time.
I scold at my preposterous notions of pride.
Do I really think that I'm supposed to get what I want.
Nothing is guaranteed
I always KNEW that!
And it makes me sick to think about
all the people that I respect that NEVER give up,
when I can't seem to do anything but anymore.
And that's what I must admit now.
I have given up.
I have completely given up
on any hope of me finding someone,
or being happy.
I can't even imagine it anymore
even fantasies seem too unrealistic.
I no longer know why I get up in the morning
I no longer do anything save for habit.

LET'S GO FOR A WALK

And I know that it's depressing to admit.
And I don't even know why I'm admitting it.
I don't know why I feel such a pressing desire
to be vulnerable in front of people.
It's like I just need to show you where I've been beaten,
and make you look at it
make you look at all the scars that the world has inflicted on me
make you face what I can't seem to look away from.
But it's so dumb
I have not suffered nearly as much as some.
I've been blessed with a lot of good things.
And am not deserving of calling what I feel pain.
Because pain seems like a full word,
a word with just as many meanings
and all interpretations,
as much as other general words
like love and hate.
It means one thing, it means all things.
I just don't understand me at all anymore.
I don't understand why I keep myself
locked away from good things.
Why can't I remember where the key is,
and even if I found it again,
would I be brave enough to unlock the door.
So I judge myself, and listen
to my off-beat thoughts
along with my accelerated heart of nicotine and caffeine.
And I watch the flickering screens
that have warm eyes and people smiling.
And I laugh with them in an absolute delirious fervor.

LET'S GO FOR A WALK

2013

LET'S GO FOR A WALK
01/06/2013

Life is full of inconsistencies.
We travel along a long road
of wavering possibilities.
The desire to no longer be fruitful
in our causes,
to meander in meaning,
to create something only known to the individual being.
When I was younger I used to think that I would eventually know
who I am, what I want, and what to do.
But the older I get the more those questions become irrelevant.
The universe doesn't work that way.
It's not about what you want,
it's about what you want at any given moment
everything is in constant flux.
If I am a man that evolves,
then what I want must always change.

And that's where you come in.
The one constant.
And every time I promise not to write about you,
the thought of your hair and eyes
sneaks through my fingertips.

But it's been a year now.
A year since I declared that I have to move on.
A year since I last heard your voice.
But my heart can't carry through the wind like it used to
now that your voice is no longer the star of my ear drums,
and I can't forget the sunshine hair that stuck to my passenger seat car
on beautiful summer days driving to the beach with the windows down.

LET'S GO FOR A WALK

The eyes that enraptured me.
The arms that held me close when I least expected them to.
The chills down my spine that one time you kissed my neck
when you were leaving me again.

And now, a week after New Years day,
a week after new beginnings and resolutions declared
you call me and I don't pick up.
I want to hear your voice more than anything in the world,
and I can't.
Because I know if I say yes to you once,
I'll never say no to you again.

You leave no voicemail,
which leaves me convinced that you called to hear my voice say,
if nothing else then,
"this is Jon's phone…leave a message."
Perhaps, you've forgotten about
the three-hour-long CD
that I made for you,
of me reading Whitman's "Song of Myself"
so you wouldn't miss me as much
when you left for Africa for 2 years.
Or perhaps you lied to me
when you said you hadn't lost it.

I have to keep reminding myself of all the times you left.
I have to keep reminding myself of all the men you fucked
while you told me you loved me.
I have to remind myself of all the crap I took to be with you,
and the life I'd take to end with you.

LET'S GO FOR A WALK

But to continue "Buggerin' on"
(as Churchill would say),
my desires must change direction.
So I have to look elsewhere.
You may listen to my voice now,
but I will no longer speak.

LET'S GO FOR A WALK

02/02/2013

Who can I trust?
Trust is one of those words that everyone seems to *think*
they know what it means,
but when you actually ask them
they're not so sure.
To me,
trust is directly linked to loyalty
I will trust you if I feel that you will have my back
that you will be there when I am down
that if I need help you will provide it for me.

But, we live in a world of actors.
Too many people that show a façade
the lies of society seeping out of the porous city sewers like sweat.
The most dangerous lies are those that the liar believes himself.

And, so, how do I even have an honest to good conversation knowing that.
Too many times, the past year or two,
my mouth has stayed shut
because I know I'll speak the truth,
and I know you'll respond with something that sounds like it.

So, how do I tell?
Well, I think it comes down to the usual instinctual things
the main tell is the eyes
I know it sounds cliché
but I can always tell from eyes
even when logic tries to play games with me
you're not looking at me right
and therefore I don't believe you.

LET'S GO FOR A WALK

But when someone is honest
when I look into those eyes
my heart warms
and I smile.

Every day I go to work
and I sit with liars,
and with truthers
funny to just realize that there's no one word
for honest people
And ALL of them say that they're my friend,
that they care about me,
even some say that they love me
but when it comes lunch time
I am not asked to go with them,
when I need a raise
I am not offered one,
when they are throwing parties
I am not invited
but when they need a web app done in 7 hours,
I'm their best fucking friend.

So, it's the truthers that deliver
Ask me how I'm doing *and* listen for the answer,
try to move things around a bit
so I can make some extra money on some projects,
and genuinely invite me out
So, that's part of trust...delivering on promises
And yes, I consider every word a promise
and yes I have very high standards on what people should live up to
once they've said something
But *that* is how you *earn* my trust.

LET'S GO FOR A WALK

02/17/2013

What makes a friendship?
How does it come about?
When I think of my friends,
the ones that have remained,
the ones who have stood trial by me and of me,
the ones that love has conquered envy, anger, and skepticism
There is no thing that made me all of a sudden realize
that they were my friend,
it's always been just the knowledge itself.
I either know you're my friend,
or I know that you're not.
There's no real deciding factor.
It's just like any sort of love,
it's something you feel.
Sure trust, loyalty, etc.
factor in
but it's really about knowing one another
on a deeper level.
So then what ends a friendship?
Is it really only when the trust goes away?
If you no longer trust someone does that *really* mean
that the friendship is over?
Because I don't think so
not anymore.
Although I no longer trust some
that I've called my friends
my love for them
is something that still stands.
Even after years of not talking,

LET'S GO FOR A WALK

if they asked me to
I would still be there for them.
I don't know if that makes me weak.
I don't know if that makes me a fool.
I just know that it's Truth.

I'm exhausted of thinking about intangible things.
I'm exhausted of thinking about Love, and Friendship, and Trust,
and Loyalty, and Truth.
What the fuck do these words mean anyway!?
They're not things you can touch, or see, or point out in any material way.
They are only feelings,
chemical reactions to things the conscious mind does not seem to grasp.
But I know when I'm without it.
I know when I'm jealous that others have it.
I know when it's present,
and I feel its loss more than fire more than a slice of a knife.

And my soul burns to touch you,
to even be friends with someone that Hot.
And, I know that it sounds perverse
and I know that Icarus loses his wings every time.
But I'm tired of being bound by land
it is time to fly if even to fall.

And I don't know how you think of me
I don't know if you're jealous of me,
envy me, desire me, are indifferent to me.
I don't know why I keep jumping back and forth
between desiring your friendship, and desiring more.
I don't know why I keep projecting rejection.
I don't know why I don't bother to feed my hungers.

LET'S GO FOR A WALK

I don't know why that destiny
seems both real, tangible, and illusory
such as love, such as trust, such as friendship.

All I know is I'm here
and I like you
and we should hang out sometime.

Soldier of Light
(02/26/2013)

We all thought he'd just get over it.
We all thought that it was wrapped up,
all the loose-ends tied,
all the meandering roads
led to the same destination.
But life is more complicated than that.
Life is *always* more complicated than that.

Walking around with loose change in my pocket
I always say to myself that it's for laundry day.
But, I have more loose change than I could ever possibly need for laundry!
But that's how life works,
we keep adding up and adding up
stories, experiences,
the good, the bad,
we anticipate that one day
it'll all gel and it'll all be spent
and so we hold onto every penny
like it's the most valuable thing in the world
just cause one day it *might* be.
But now I have too many jars filled with quarters,
and they just sit there.

But old habits die hard,
and his emotions got the best of him.
His emotions were built up
too many jars of change
and he kept harboring them,
thinking it was the useful thing to do.

LET'S GO FOR A WALK

But closure is funny that way.
Just because you think you have money saved up,
that you've earned the right to deposit your coins in the slot,
doesn't mean that the machine isn't going to
just spit your quarter right back out.

We all thought he was over it.
The trauma, the battle scars, the betrayals,
the women who lied to him, the patriarchs that abandoned him
we all thought he got passed it all
we all thought he had a chance for a 'normal' life now.

But it's not that easy,
it's *never* that easy
And now his fury is unleashed
no longer quite human
no longer quite anything but confusion.

Walking around the battlefield,
having conversations of what it means to have a rational thought
what it means to be crazy
what it means to believe in something with no proof,
but still have no faith.

Desperate for human affections,
no longer privy to the Gods' intentions
praying to be knocked off his feet
never earth bound always in the ethereal
the only path to redemption is for the battle to change,
for war to change,
but change is hard to come by.

LET'S GO FOR A WALK

So I give him a smile,
throw him a coin,
and go on my merry way.
Today is just another day to be in the realm of disbelief.
Today is just another day to say what we mean.
Today is just another day, another way, another possibility
of 'getting over it'.

Secret Poem

I have no desire to 'seize the day',
I merely wish to accompany it.
Watch a movie, play a video game,
read some *poems*.
Everyone goes on and on about how 'life is short',
but I say life is long.
Take your time.
What's the rush?
Remember when we were young
and the idea that we'd live to be 100 years, or 80 years,
or even that we'd live to be 20
seemed like infinity?
Well, remind yourself of that
fore life is only as long as you let it be.
So let's relax, enjoy ourselves, have some drinks,
and remember that sometimes
in fact even if it's more than sometimes
it's fine
even encouraged
to sleep the weekend away.

LET'S GO FOR A WALK
03/11/2013

If you see a loner,
you take him in.
That's what I've always done.
Is it that strange of me to expect the same of others?
There is a severe importance to not *let* people be alone.
We, as a culture,
romanticize the idea of the 'lone wolf',
but in truth
in the wild
the lone wolf's likelihood of survival is slim.
So take him in,
and give him shelter.
Become a friend,
and don't *let* him be alone.
We hunt together, we die together,
we fight together, we love together
that is what we've been designed to do.
It is only when we've lost hope
that we end up *wanting* to be alone,
I see it almost as nature's self-destruct mechanism
Since we are pack animals,
if the pack has rejected us,
then we have no reason to survive.
Which is why loneliness leads to depression,
loneliness leads to madness,
loneliness leads to suicide.
So if you see a lone wolf
do not *let* him be alone.

LET'S GO FOR A WALK

I've been in this city for over a year now.
I've walked the streets alone.
I've worked and eaten and loved and fought by myself.
Every now and then to lend some words,
every now and then to reconnect with an old companion
I've ventured out.
But I do not understand this city.
I do not understand it's people,
and perhaps it's that I don't understand people in general
whenever I've seen someone alone I don't *let* him be.
But here,
it seems there are very few inviting me in.
They see me alone
and think it better to let be
they don't trust
so they don't engage.
I don't trust,
so I attempt to learn more about what I don't understand
which makes me even stranger to them.
I know that I'm strange.
I know that the lone wolf seems more dangerous
than one with a pack
but can't you understand
that's why I'm trying to find one?
I am not desperate
I'm just attempting to avoid insanity.

When I began writing poetry again,
I promised myself something.
That I must be truthful.
I must be as absolutely honest as possible.
Don't sugar coat.

LET'S GO FOR A WALK

Don't whine.
Don't command.
Don't be anything but explanatory and legitimate
no matter the embarrassment,
no matter if it sounds wrong
because it *always* will
no matter the grammar
no matter if it's an actual sentence
no matter if you're the 'lone wolf',
or if I'm the 'lonewolf'
no matter perspective or pronoun
no matter if rhyme *or* reason...

But if you feel alone in this world
you *must* say it
and mean it
and understand it
and teach it
because it is a feeling
because if I'm not trying to figure all this out
then there's absolutely no reason to write poetry
or anything at all
and if there's nothing to write about,
if there's nothing to learn and try to understand anymore
then fucking kill me now because I've learned it all
and I'm not even fucking 30!!

So yes,
today, this year this fucking era
I've been the lone wolf
and fuck you guys for not throwing me a bone.

Sipping on wine trying not to complain
(03/16/2013)

The trick is to catch a passing thought.
The trick is to snatch it before it slips away
into the crevices of consciousness it came from.
My thoughts are *always* scattered.
I've been trying to gather them up
in a basket and make some logic from them.
But I always seem to drop
one while picking up another,
one by one frantically trying to get them all in.
Trying to understand it all.
Trying to understand the process of contemplation.
The litany of frustration
I feel when trying to organize.
The adjustments I have to make to my personality.
I can no longer be so emotional.
I can no longer feel before I think.
I need to make money.
I need to talk to people.
I need to be a member of society.
But my mind won't seem to let me.
It shuts others out.
It shuts *me* out.
My mind has a mind of its own.

Up all night talking to a friend about my problems.
It felt so juvenile.
I have the crazy inclination that I'm too old to have problems.
Or at least by 28 I should no longer feel such a *need* to talk about them.
Again, my mind not making sense

LET'S GO FOR A WALK

again feeling like I should somehow be doing 'better' than I am.
Listening to people walk by my window.
They laugh.
They drink.
They seem to be having a good time.
I could join them.
All I'd have to do is wash, clothe, and walk somewhere.
But something keeps me locked inside my apartment.
Something tells me I can't handle the outside.
Something tells me it's safer here.
Something is lying it's ass off to me.
But again I realize that it's me.
But how do you refute yourself?

Sipping on wine trying not to complain.
I'm hungry, I'm lonely, I'm horny!

Knowing to solve this
I should eat something good
and fuck someone good.
But alcohol seems an easy substitute for both.

Another lazy Saturday night where nothing happens.
Another night filled with desires unfulfilled.
Another night of fantasies.
Another night of
possible movies, and possible women, and possible bars.
Another night of
actual writing, of actual video games, of actual internet browsing.
Staying quarantined to my home,
out of fear that my confusion is contagious.

So I finish my glass, and decide, I might do something later.

LET'S GO FOR A WALK

03/25/2013

1.

Spending most of my days sipping on nostalgia,
I walk around with air in my heart and blood in my lungs.
Desperately trying to awaken the fruit fly of emotion
that transpires to the dark recession of the moon's eye.
I walk around with a desire
to freak-out at the slightest stir of bonding
and freestyle my mind to spin in circles
til the never-ending kaleidoscope of thought designates
that an end is near.
We can no longer presume that death is an illusion.
We can no longer understand what it means
to sin without accepting that Hell might await us,
and sex and love and all those things that protect us
from the agonies of arrival to the best idea
that we are not alone in this world
that we suffer for no one but ourselves
that we are at last the least annoying
the absolute most enduring
the greatest thing that ever existed
the dying delight of passive integrity
the illusory light of the red carpet.
The building of swaying
the wetness of anxious awakening
the thrust of life exiting and entering.
I keep sending interpreting the air.
I keep letting myself understand the unseen.
I keep listening. I am listening.

LET'S GO FOR A WALK

2.

The fruit of our labors can not justify the end.
The justification only happens
when the herbs can mingle with the spices.
When the salt of the earth
meets the pepper of spacious delightful gardens.
The tongue is just another organ
that wishes to move and delight
with sultry appetite.

And I have no fucking clue what these songs mean.
These songs that come to me in my dreams.
These lyrical embassies to realms unseen.
These lyrical quandaries to questions never asked.

And I wonder where it ends,
and I wonder what it means to 'happen',
when what's happening to me is not an action
is not an experience
when what happens to me
is something transitional
and just that like seasons changing
both a multitude of chain reactions
but only the perception that
today I woke up and it is warm,
when yesterday was cold.

And I wonder where it ends
and I wonder when I close my eyes what remains
just words and light.
That's all that exists now
words and light.

LET'S GO FOR A WALK
04/01/2013

Today, on the way to lunch,
walking and speaking with coworkers and friends
I spotted a dead man on the corner
being helped to some CPR.
I say spotted,
because I only turned my head for a moment.
Validating what I saw
with my companions,
we soldiered on
trying to recover a previous mood
of delight on a beautiful Spring day.

"Life is too short", people have told me.
But some lives are longer than others.
Some lives are fuller than others.
Some lives are happier
My point is
that life and length
are relative words.
How long was this man's life
and how much life did he live?
Is it terrible that me,
a complete stranger,
walked by only shaken
enough to say a few words
before focusing on the food
I was about to purchase and consume
the food that man obviously didn't have nearly enough of.

LET'S GO FOR A WALK

One question is,
"why do I feel so bad about a dead stranger?"
The other question being,
"why don't I feel worse?"

These are feelings and questions
that I have the luxury to ponder
in my warm Astoria apartment
sipping on wine.
And I wish I could write about this man
even describe what he looked like,
but I could only tell a couple of things.

He wore that gray
you know the poor-man's uniform
that gray that they all wear
that gray that you have the slightest notion
may have once been another color.

His legs were apart, and his neck was wrong
too much to the left to be in a position to be breathing.

Then he was just feet to me
then he was something I saw.

And so,
since I can't speak of him,
I speak of myself
using him as a vehicle for writing.
It's almost disgusting to me.
It's almost wrong
but enough alright
to keep doing it.

LET'S GO FOR A WALK

I've been watching The Twilight Zone lately.
I've been watching it not only with sight and sound but with Mind.
And it sticks with you.
In fact I think I've been watching it my entire existence.
Starting when I was 3-years-old
and remembering my first nightmare
of a giant blue cat that killed my parents.
Continuing on to Elementary school
where I was beaten up by children
who claimed to be my friends.
Later to High School and college
when I fell into a crowd of strange people,
who believed in magic and spells and The Earth and the Darkness
and Light and how it all seemed one to them
yet they dispersed like an atom
exploding all across the globe
leaving, Me, the nucleus remaining.

And now,
how I go through my day
walking by those
dying on the streets.
How I spend my nights
mingling with the underground cultures,
to come to light and laugh
with the mainstream.
I realize now and again
that there's nothing that separates us
that if you see a dead man
it sticks with you
that it is the one thing that we all have in common.

LET'S GO FOR A WALK

05/11/2013

Frustration with the satisfaction
of knowing
that this isn't what I dreamed about.
That the dream
is a reality unto itself.
That the desire
to escape
surpasses
the desire
to embrace.

I write gibberish.
I can't articulate my feelings
in a rational way,
so I attempt to jumble words together
frantically trying to express
something I can't make sense of.
My grandfather is dying,
and I won't accept it.
He is 94-years-old
and the most brilliant man I've ever known,
and slowly throughout the past three years
his mind has been dwindling
to the point where he doesn't always know
who I am anymore
or who he is
or anyone.
It hurts to try to understand,
to accept that my times with him
of being his student,

LET'S GO FOR A WALK

of being his grandson
are over.
Now I am just some guy in the room,
and he has lost the spark he once had
Sometimes it returns though.
Sometimes I catch a glimpse
of the man he once was,
and he knows me
and for five minutes
I'm a teenager again
drinking in with fervor
all the wisdom he has
to bestow on me
and then,
moments later,
I'm a stranger
and so is he
and I don't know how to describe
how it feels to love someone
who doesn't know you.
I don't know how to express that.
I don't know how to comprehend it.

And I'm tired of this city's weather
I want it to decide
whether it's hot or cold,
just like I want my grandfather's mind to decide
whether it exists or not.
I want people in this city
to open up
and embrace me,
because I can't go on

LET'S GO FOR A WALK

much longer
feeling this way
without anyone to hold onto.

But people can't embrace what they don't see.
And, this constant struggle of trying to reveal myself,
in a world that favors seclusion and secrets
that rewards those who lack emotion,
that punishes the sensitive
and favors Pride, Elegance, and Self-Admiration
has led me to be quiet,
and has forced me to the corners of rooms
trying to blend in.

And I'm tired of wanting
does that make any fucking sense,
I'm tired of wanting altogether
because it's disgusting
I have SO MUCH
I am not hungry.
I am not living on the streets.
But I'm never happy.
I'm never satisfied.
I don't think I've always been this way
and yeah, fuck it, I blame society.
I was NOT built for this capitalist man eat man culture we live in.
But I also can't imagine myself living in some commune
where everyone pretends to love each other.
So where the fuck do I fit into this mess?
What the hell is it that I'm looking for?
I thought I had found someone
that could make me happy.

LET'S GO FOR A WALK

But it ended up that she was a dream as well
just the most vivid.

And I'm tired of all the flaky people in my life,
and I'm extremely angry that I've become one.

And I'm tired of all the people that care only enough to seem like they do.

And I'm tired of judging people, and feeling judged.

And I'm tired of all the cravings.

And I'm tired of wanting sex.

And I'm tired of wanting to hear a good story so I could sleep.

And I'm tired of struggling for rent.

And I'm tired of wanting a Cat...just a cat,
I grew up with cats,
but now I can't even afford one.

And I'm tired of thinking I'm not good enough for this world.

And I'm tired of worrying about my job,
and constantly feeling like I'll be fired any day now
and have to move back home to start over once again.

But most of all
I wish I could talk to him about all these things.
Because he always knew what to say.
But now he could barely remember.
His wisdom is lost.
Now I am on my own and I'm not ready for it,
and I don't know if or when I will be.

LET'S GO FOR A WALK

Lost in my emotions
with no one to guide me through it anymore.
I'm tired of having this sadness.
I'm tired of wanting someone to take it from me,
when I know that's not possible.

So, what is there left to do?
I'm asking you,
what is there left for me to do?

The heat is overwhelming me.
The suffocation of my emotions
and the intense stink of dying desperation.
It's gross
the sadness is vomit-inducing.
It's poison
the slowest working poison there is.
Someday I'll either be rid of it,
or I will be consumed by it.
But to not fight,
would be the greatest betrayal
of the lessons he has taught me.
So it is my responsibility
to continue the battle,
to continue arguing with myself
and proving that I am worthy of saying
that I was a student of Leonard Cherlin,
that I was his grandson,
and that he was my friend.
And, although he might not remember himself anymore,
I always will.

LET'S GO FOR A WALK

06/10/2013

1.

I don't understand the hostility
that results
from any time I ever ask a question.
In my opinion,
if you get angry
whenever someone questions your beliefs,
then I am right to assume
that you don't believe it enough to defend it.
Likewise,
if you get angry
when someone questions your knowledge,
then I am right to assume
that you don't actually know what you're talking about.

Sure, we live in a world
of Google and Wikipedia.
So information is available and plenty.
But what always comes to mind
is the lessons that my grandfather told me.
He used to give me clarinet lessons.
During these lessons,
he would give me an assignment
that I should only play two lines of a piece
over and over for an hour each day.
He would specifically tell me *not* to go ahead
and try everything else,
because I had to master these two lines first.
But I would get impatient many times,

and try to jump ahead.
When I did this
he would always know,
and would tell me,
"Now you learned it wrong.
Now it will take you two weeks to learn it right.
One week to unlearn what you learned wrong
and one week to learn it the right way."

So with the lavish amount of information on the Internet
there is a high possibility
of learning something wrong.
That's why I prefer to ask experts,
or have them point me in the right direction.
But often times these so-called "experts"
get offended by this.
Which is something I don't understand.

To ask a question
is to not assume an answer.
The desire to pursue curiosities
is natural and should never be punished.
If you have ever reprimanded someone
for asking a question
then you are an enemy to knowledge.

LET'S GO FOR A WALK

2.

"I will be moving out of state in two months.
Wanted to know
if you would like to meet up
for coffee or something
at some point
before I leave."

This is the text
that is currently on my phone.
The text I received
while I was in the shower
Monday morning,
the first day of my vacation.
The text is from a girl
and I use the word girl purposefully,
as we are not describing a woman
a woman has maturity and dignity
a girl is still stunted
in being only obsessed
with getting what she wants.

This girl
is the only person
I have ever truly said and meant
that I am in love with.
And, yes,
I mean that in the present tense
because love is an addiction
and just like an alcoholic is always an alcoholic
no matter how long he goes without a drop

LET'S GO FOR A WALK

I am in love with Rachel.

I try to towel myself off
and focus on the rest of the day
the plans I had to catch up with an old friend
the inevitable glee
that I will get from reading
about the video game expo that starts today.
But that text those words
that knowledge that in two months
she'll be actually out of reach again...

It's been over a year and a half now
since I told her that we can not be friends anymore.
It had been 10 years of me torturing myself
always wanting her, and being rejected.
This girl plays with the emotions of men,
and seduces the bodies of boys.
This girl who can make a man feel complete
and then ridicule him for it.

I meet with a friend
and sip on bubble tea
while discussing the nature of society
and the ridiculousness of capitalism
and working oneself to exhaustion.
She is an old friend from my time in college
wonderful and beautiful
I always question why
I never fell in love with her.
Again, is it that I seem to have this never-ending desire
to take something that could be simple

LET'S GO FOR A WALK

and over-complicate it.

I walk around Chinatown
catching up with my friend
but Rachel is never far from my mind
her text in my pocket
waiting to be answered.
My bones telling me
to see her again,
my heart freaking out
because it has been so long without a fix.
And I can't breathe anymore.
I can't see anymore
I no longer hear the conversation I am participating in.
I hear Rachel
I recall her voice
and her eyes
and her hair
and that feeling of completion
and forget the pain
and the lies
and the cruelties that she wilfully inflicted on me.

I imagine that I won't answer the text.

All the times I wanted to grab her, kiss her
All those women I grabbed and kissed and wished it was her.
But y'know
I'm tired of writing about her.
She is not the main focus of my life.
She can't be.
If there is ever happiness

then it is not being obsessed with a girl
that doesn't understand how I feel.
A girl that is obsessed with me loving her,
but could never return it.

And the idea that this is still a thing,
is a sickness.
The idea that she is the only one that I want still,
is a tragic circumstance.
My words hold me back,
I am not letting myself know the true nature of things.
I am the one lighting the fire and reciprocating the flame.

Semi-Autobiographic-Commentary
(06/17/2013)

My time
has a fractured continuity.

I once had a "revelation"
only to find
a few days later
an old notebook
where I had stated the exact same "revelation"
five years before.
I have since forgotten what it was.

I will always be clumsy.
My body matches my mind
in the sense that I am always off-balance
and trying to find my footing.
Always off-beat,
and trying to find my rhythm.

Maybe it's an inner-ear thing.
Maybe that's why I'm always so loud.

I consistently feel
a yearning for self exploration
to understand myself
to a degree
that is in actuality
impossible.
I have no secrets
because I have no time for them.
Many people

seem to mistake insecurity
and self-abashedness,
for someone who is mysterious.
But true mystery
is when the picture is in front of you,
but you just can't quite make out what it's of.

Time floats.
It is lighter than air.
It is above space and below it.
And time goes through us.
We are only conduits.
I was born
and as a child
I had bicycles,
I had pets,
I had family,
I had friends
some of those things
have been passed on,
some passed away,
some still remain.
But I have no control over it.

I constantly battle
to hold onto some semblance of rationality,
some sort of logic
some rules of causality.
But the truth is
that one thing does not cause another
but instead many things cause many things
and all at the same moment

LET'S GO FOR A WALK

the nature of reality is like a pulse
a word that is singular
but requires more than one beat.

And again I know that none of this makes sense.
Again I know that my logic seems flawed,
that the ideas I have
are always contradictory.

I want to fuck, but I'm scared of embracing.

I want to eat, but I'm afraid to get fat.

I want to write, but don't believe it will mean anything.

I want to drink, but am too tired to drink too much.

Always desires, then fears
when life might be more productive the other way around.

But it's not my nature.

Again, constantly lazy but always need to take the more difficult route.

Nothing being easy. Always in flux.

Always uncomfortable and awkward.

Watching people laugh and bend,
when I instead
cower in a corner
observing their dance of equanimity.

And when I looked at her she lit up the room.
Her being so beautiful

LET'S GO FOR A WALK

and strong-minded
and strong-willed
did not seem fair to the rest of the human race.
So I decided to avoid her
because the moment she felt I wanted her
she'd know she had me
and I couldn't allow myself to be had again.

I once read to a girl a line I had written for another girl

"...The one with the eyes I could drown in,
fore while staring into their deep angelic beauty,
I might forget to breathe..."

She said,
"Now I'll just imagine you wrote that for me."
I didn't.
And, I didn't claim that I did.
And she was a much better person than the girl I wrote it for.

And that about sums it up doesn't it.
Always falling for the wrong girl,
and never pursuing the right one.
Jumping in and out of the game.
Sometimes watching,
sometimes participating,
but always confused.

The clock ticks somewhere,
but I no longer understand what it measures.
I'm a child. I'm in love.
I'm an adult. I'm telling her I can never speak to her again.
I walk into a room where everyone knows my name.

LET'S GO FOR A WALK

I sit in my apartment crying to cope with a sunny day.

And yes I prefer the rain,
and always have.
And my mother would chase me
as I would run out of the house to play in it
only 4-years-old
and felt more at peace with gray clouds than with white ones.

But now it doesn't make sense.
It seems more like a semi-bio for a character in a story,
than being a story itself.

But in order for this be done it must be over and therefore must end.

So I'll leave you with this...

If a tree falls in the forest,
what came first
the tree,
or the inevitability of the fall?

LET'S GO FOR A WALK
09/02/2013

I keep waiting for the day
when Doc Brown is going to take me away
in his time machine.
I grew up with wonderful stories.
Stories of time-travel, space-travel
stories of adventure, romance, and action.
I keep waiting for my adventure to begin.
I keep waiting for the moment
when someone tells me
that I'm special,
and everything I've experienced
up to this point
suddenly makes sense.
I grew up with stories about heroes.

But now
I'm almost 30
and my travels amount
to moving out of my home
and attempting to make a new one
in the same state
on the same land-mass
in a different county.

I have yet to leave this country once.
I instead put a hold on travels
in order to find some sort of self-sufficiency and financial footing.
But my therapist tells me I'm depressed.
And how dare he tell me that.
I know the signs of depression.

LET'S GO FOR A WALK

Heck I minored in Psychology.
How could I get depressed?
I was always the one getting people out of depression.
I mean sure I've lost interest in things,
and I don't socialize much,
and I've put on some weight,
and I've felt sort of uninspired to write,
and....hmmm.

Self-realizations piss me off.
It's incredibly annoying
when you find out that you've fallen into
exactly what you spent so much effort
steering away from.

And now when I watch my favorite movies and favorite shows,
of my past,
it reminds me of what I thought my life would be
what I knew my life would be
what I wanted from my life,
and who I thought I was.

I thought I was a hero.
I thought I was an adventurer.
I thought of myself as a romantic.
I thought of myself as a man of action.
But I've proven to be a coward.
I've taken the safe route.
I'm terrified of intimacy.
I lay around watching Netflix on hot summer weekend nights,
when I should be out finding things to write about.

And I'm jealous of those who write about being right.

LET'S GO FOR A WALK

I'm jealous of the confidence that they have of "knowing" anything
the confidence they have to see in black and white,
good and bad
the pride they take in their words.

Doubt is an anesthetic.
It numbs the mind. It numbs the heart.
And protects them from pain, but also from touch.

And *God* it's been awhile.
God I miss sex.
And, yes,
it's been long enough for me to miss it.
The teasing and comforting
the rising and falling
the aggression and sympathy
the conversation between bodies
the competition on who gets who to submit first.

But in order to pursue a mate,
I need to remember who I am.
I need to know what it is I have to offer.
I need to find that hero in me.
I need to remind myself of my dreams as a child.
And although life has felt long,
I'm still told I'm young.
I need this to be a stage,
and for my future to be a life.

Feelin' Groovy
(09/25/2013)

Sometimes I wish I could just steal lyrics
from Simon and Garfunkel songs.
I want to be able to say that
I'm "Feelin' Groovy" or that
"I am a Rock, I am an Island".
But these are words that don't belong to me.
But isn't that strange
that someone could own a string of words.
Someone can own a melody,
it's almost like saying that
someone can own an emotion.

Which leads me to remembering
a scene in Metal Gear Solid,
where they are talking about
how you can't record a memory.
That memories are too complex,
laced with emotions and perspectives
that no matter how far technology comes
we'll never be able to capture such things.
But I think about
how a little over 100 years ago,
people would think it impossible
to record moving pictures that also spoke
that it would seem just as impossible
as recording a thought or an emotion.
So, I think that's the next step
that soon we will be able to record our memories,
our emotions,

LET'S GO FOR A WALK

our dreams.
And then, in turn,
they will no longer be 'ours'.
I mean maybe we could have a patent on them
such as on a lyric in a song
but they will no longer solely belong to us.
Everyone will be able to interpret and take from it,
whatever their perspectives add to it.

And dreams...

As of now, no one knows what a dream really is.
We know that our minds,
often cannot tell the difference between dreams and reality
while we are experiencing it.
We perceive the dream as we perceive reality.
We accept the occurrences of a dream
as we accept the occurrences of the real.
So, perhaps there isn't much of a difference at all.
And therefore,
in the future,
when we no longer own our dreams
will we also
no longer own our realities?
Or, is that already so?

We share on facebook,
we tweet on twitter,
and we are ALWAYS linked in.
We no longer own our realities
we merely have a patent on them.

LET'S GO FOR A WALK

However,
I don't know if this is completely a negative thing.
I've always said,
that if we are ever going to be united in peace,
that we must first learn how to understand each other
communicate with each other.
So isn't this the way to do that?
If we can see each other's thoughts,
and feel each other's emotions
won't we understand?
Or is understanding completely separate from that?
Is understanding something else?
After all, I rarely understand my own emotions,
so why should I understand yours?

And what of secrets?
I've always despised secrets, even my own.
But there are times that I feel they're necessary
at least to maintain the status quo
at least to hold back change.
If I told you my secrets, there's no way you'd see me the same
I'd be different to you
I'd be something else, and you might not like that,
and I might seem even more vulnerable more scared more deranged
than you've anticipated.

My emotions are swirling, and I wish to express them, but to do so reveals secrets, and therefore it's an endless vortex spinning into the eternal quagmire of space and sound and light and energy but somehow centrifugally spreading out gliding towards you.

Layers and layers of whatness of fullness

LET'S GO FOR A WALK

of emptiness of laughter and crying
of devouring soul-driving
careening towards the exit never ceasing to participate
in the grand scheme
the irony of falling while moving
forward in a dream.

And I feel light-headed numbness from the caffeine
of this afternoon's coffee.
I am lost in the fantasies of time-travel-surrealistic-dream-world-epidemic-science-fiction.

But I'm walking along singing:

"...hello lamp-post, what ya knowin',

I've come to watch your flowers growin'

Ain't ya got no rhymes for me,

do-it-do-do,

feelin' groovy

LA LA LA LA

feelin' groovy..."

LET'S GO FOR A WALK
09/30/2013

It's exhausting isn't it?

Trying to put these feelings into words.
Trying to stop a minute to articulate the sensation.

Sometimes I need a lubricant
and not necessarily the dirty kind
but of the alcoholic variety.

Because when you can't fuck,
you might as well drink,
and the constant temptations when being a single male.

I leave out the word young,
because I no longer know what that means,
or if I should identify with it,
or if I really ever have.

I recall my father once telling me
that I was a 40-year-old in an 8-year-old body.
I've never been truly reckless
sure with a heart or two
but never really dove into anything without thinking it over first
no matter if I was right or wrong
in predicting the outcome.
I envy that.
I've always envied those that don't require contemplation
to make the decisions,
but instead do.
Sure they experience a lot of drama.
But they also seem so alive, passionate, and engaged.

LET'S GO FOR A WALK

They're not detached from everything.
They don't seem as disconnected as I feel.
But the grass is always greener right?
The grass...
My roommate recently explained to me
that I should stop trying to analyze everything
because sometimes the "grass is just green".
I replied with,
"But the grass is green for a reason."
I'm sure though he was making the allusion
to that sometimes
"a cigar is just a cigar",
not some phallic symbol.
I guess my reply to that
would have been that a
"cigar is a cigar for a reason"
and perhaps that people put it in their mouths, and puff,
is not just a coincidence.

And so I go on smoking my seasonal cigarettes.
Breathe in chemicals...exhale essence.
The air is not quite biting enough for my liking yet
and I yearn for the contemplative relaxation
of knowing that through the snow was a destination.
I remember walking to her house.
I remember her refusing to see me.
I, trying to make art out of disillusion
and she trying to forget how easy it had been for me
to dismiss her feelings as a ridiculous crush.
I'm sorry Krystal,
I wish I could say that once and have you truly hear it.
You will forever be my 'what if'.

LET'S GO FOR A WALK

Anyway, I wonder what my point will be this time,
I mean every story, every poem, every god damned thing I say
always has a point or two or three or fucking infinite amounts of wisdom,
or whatever I think might be
wise / meaningful / make something make sense!

But perhaps tonight there is no point.
Just the drunken ramblings of a guy desperately trying to make one.

And again I think how I should be happy with the life I live.
How lucky I am.
How so fucking privileged I am to be here, not poor, not starving,
just here and living comfortably in my Astoria apartment.
But I'm never truly satisfied
and I know I'm not ever supposed to be
but god damned why does my destiny feel so itchy,
like I'm always having to scratch it
hoping that the bleeding will make it stop
but it doesn't and I keep scratching until I hit bone and cartilage
never truly arriving at a release
but instead exacting more and more pain every time I try.

And I wish I had more time.
I always wish I had more time to just, figure this out.
But the timer's ticking and it can't stop, it won't stop,
like some modern pop song on crack.

But it doesn't matter.

Even though time continues, I won't.
This thought will end
all thoughts I have will eventually halt.
Time keeps ticking but my ticker won't be wound.

I just hope I leave some resonance,
some totality,
some sort of constant associated with something that relates to me
once I step away from the stage.
But even if I do,
I'll never really know it.

So this minute, like all minutes, end.

So, did I articulate the sensation?

A World Where Being Against a Term Contributes to the Problem
(10/13/2013)

I am a heterosexual male.
I am told that I am a part of "Rape Culture",
even though I respect women,
promote female equality,
encourage women to pursue their dreams
even in careers that are not traditionally women-friendly
(such as science, math, and tech-related industries),
and even *actually* stopped a close friend of mine
from killing herself after she was brutally raped.
I was there for her.
I was there when she was in so much pain
that she couldn't sit down / lie down / stand.
So I held her as she cried on my shoulder asking me "why".

However, if I am horny,
and a girl walks by with a great ass,
and I check her out,
and she happens to see my eyes
looking at said ass
no matter if I was trying to be subtle
and if she is uncomfortable with that
then I am contributing to a
male-dominated female-subjugated society
that encourages men to rape.
If I laugh at a joke that is deemed sexist or derogatory
well that also encourages men to rape.
If I watch porn, listen to a song that has the word "bitch",

LET'S GO FOR A WALK

and have a private conversation
with a group of guys
on what girls we would love to fuck
then I am contributing to "Rape Culture".
This seems to be the mentality of many "Feminists"
that I have read, spoken to, and overheard.
A girl I know said,
in a group conversation, that
"if you don't believe that 'Rape Culture' exists,
then I want nothing to do with you."
I announced,
that I do believe that there are problems in our society
when it comes to the treatment of women.
But I don't like the term "Rape Culture".
Arguments ensued,
and I was told that by not supporting the term
then I am contributing to the problem.
I used to refer to myself as a Feminist,
since it was presented to me as a movement
that promotes female equality.
However, Feminism seems to have devolved
into a movement that has created a world
where if a man writes a song about how he thinks a girl "wants it"
then he deserves to be villainized based on that alone
be deemed as having a hand in "Rape Culture"
again *RAPE*
an extremely horrible act of violent torture
for thinking that a woman is attracted to him.
They seem to make the jump from sexual attraction to sexual assault,
based on passing glances and words.
And I'm not condoning men who are disrespectful.

LET'S GO FOR A WALK

If a woman rejects you,
then I do not condone you calling her a bitch.
If a woman is walking by you and you are leering at her with desire
and telling her to bring her ass over to you
well then you're a creepy asshole.
However, I do not assume that you want to Rape her.
And that's the problem,
there will *ALWAYS* be assholes.
I do not think that this is a culturally specific phenomena.
It is not something that could ever be completely eradicated.
However, by promoting proper manners, education, etc.
we can decrease this.
But, we need to focus on the positive.
Deeming an entire culture as supporting rape
is daunting and extremely general.
Instead, focus on individuals, groups, even industries.
You can change a person
it takes much more time to change a culture.
Again, be proactive and not defeatest.
Don't blame society for an individuals decision
to perform a vicious act of violence.
A person must be held *personally* responsible for his or her actions.

Anyway, because of this,
I now solely identify myself as a Humanist.
One of the definitions of Humanism is the
"Interest in the welfare of people."
That's right, people!
Not just man, not just woman
people.
Men *and* women are not entitled to anything
based on their sex or gender alone.

LET'S GO FOR A WALK

All men and women are entitled to
equality and respect.
However, when we get to the point
that we can no longer speak our minds
that we feel shameful about our desires and urges
that we blame society and diminish personal responsibility
then we are no longer doing anything at all.
We are stagnant.
Because there's no place to go from there.

I am an extremely shy individual when it comes to women.
I always have been.
I find some women to be so beautiful
that at times it has taken every fiber of my being
to actually establish coherent words while facing them.
I say this
admit this to you all
because there have been times that I am so terrified
of making women feel uncomfortable and / or creeped out,
that I have literally been unable to speak.
I have thought a lot about this over the years,
and I think I'm beginning to see why I've become this way.
In the attempt to bring equality to women,
through Feminism,
there is terminology that by default villainizes men.
Even while writing this,
I am terrified.
I believe I might be even more scared when I say it aloud.
And, of course, that's the very reason I *should* say it aloud:

LET'S GO FOR A WALK

I am a heterosexual male.
I am a good man.
I do *NOT* promote rape against men or women.
I am *NOT* part of the problem.
I *AM* part of the solution.
So stop bundling me into a term
as general and unspecific as "culture".

A Saturday Night
(11/04/2013)

I sit here writing on my notepad
because my 8-month-old cat
chewed straight through my laptop's AC adapter.
This is interesting
because I can't remember
the last time that I sat down
and actually wrote down my thoughts
pen to paper...well sober at least.

Consistently my thoughts have been digitized
words broken down to pixels, broken down to numbers.

It's funny
because my words have to be
the only kind of math
that never add up.
I mean sure you could make summations and quantify,
but my words and thoughts
never have one answer to any specific equation
instead lying in the quantum of probabilities.

And I do mean "probabilities" and not "possibilities",
because anything is possible but not everything is probable
and when they tell you that
"...for each closed door another one opens..."
what they don't explain is
that each door locks from the outside,
and you can never go back.

And now I choose each thought, each word, in terror

LET'S GO FOR A WALK

which is why I prefer typing
since I can go faster,
don't have to think as much.
But, here, each mistake is final
or at the very least a big blot of crossed out scribbles.

And so I go out for a night.
I decide that there needs to be more words in my ethereal chronicle
my destiny with no destination.
And, so I base the night on a song...one of my favorites,
"One Bourbon, One Scotch, and One Beer".
I think,
"I'll make a theme of it, bar hop each round."

The first bar is crowded with young men and women
about my age but better looking.
I order my round
and tell the bartender it's based on the song
he doesn't know it
drink the bourbon, drink the scotch,
waitress tells me I'm in the way and asks me to move
as I sip on my beer and observe.

I look to my right
and see a packed table of men and women
specifically 6 men and 4 women
disproportional in the wrong way.

I look to my left and see 2 women
sitting at a table next to each other talking.
Now sitting next to each other could be purposeful
as to invite male bystanders such as myself.
However, I decide I'm not quite drunk enough yet

LET'S GO FOR A WALK

for conversation with strangers,
finish my beer, and head to the next bar.

I enter and see a couple of middle-aged men.
2 cute girls (a blonde and brunette),
at the far end of the bar,
are watching a group of young guys
at the pool table
or rather are attempting to
get the young guys
to watch them.

I sit down and order my round
the bartender says,
"Oh...like the song."

The guy next to me is another guy named John.
He's overweight and just turned 52 yesterday.
He sends a drink to the girls at the end of the bar,
as I place my face into my bourbon
hoping they don't think the bartender's finger is pointing at me
again, not drunk enough yet.

John tells me that he's an engineer
and has lived here for 15 years.
Bill (the ex-cop) comes over
and says I remind him of Elvis...
NOT the King of Rock...
but the guy who had a room in his apartment
specifically dedicated to old Playboy magazines,
and had a quadruple digit bar tab
that stopped him from going here in 2003.

LET'S GO FOR A WALK

Billy tells me about John and Elvis
tells me about running down kids with guns while on the force.
I finish my scotch, start on my beer, and begin to feel at home.

At last I am drunk enough to approach a woman.
I talk to the blonde
not because I'm a gentleman
but because she has a lip ring and a Ninja Turtles shirt
and I feel we'd have things to talk about.

I feel I am doing well.
She called me an asshole (I don't remember why),
but it probably had something to do with the muscular tan guy
whom I had interrupted her conversation with.

So, I begin talking with the brunette
and the 3 guys gathered around her.
I don't recall what we spoke of
something about music
one guy air guitars and explains to me that,
"When you see guys air guitaring like this
(he gestures with his fingers)
they probably legit know how to play."

The world is hazy now
and I start to think about my day.
A coworker of mine had shown me a YouTube video
about a guy who gets kisses from women
after asking 3 questions.
Before I know it,
I'm asking the group if they've seen this video.
I explain,
"So this guy goes up to the girls and says

LET'S GO FOR A WALK

1) 'Do you find me attractive?'
2) 'Do you have a boyfriend?'
3) 'So what's stopping you from kissing me right now?'
And before they can answer the last question,
he just kisses them!"
As I say this,
the blonde gives an over-dramatic scream.
I think she's being funny so I laugh and ask,
"So do you think that's creepy...or awesome?"
The guy sitting in front of me says,
"It's not going to be so awesome if you laugh in my ear again?"
I say,
"What? I laughed in your ear? I'm sorry man."
He looks at his friend and says,
"Hey, tell this guy what's gonna happen in 2 seconds."
And so I ask the friend (and I still can't believe I did this),
"What's gonna happen in 2 seconds?"
The guy says,
"Step outside and you'll find out,"
as the friend explains that I was hitting on this guy's girl
the blonde.
I point out that everyone's hitting on her
but that doesn't make the situation better.
Which leads to the friend forcing the guy to leave with him.

As they walk out, I ask the girl,
"Was that your boyfriend?"
She says,
"No."
But that I had really creeped her out with those questions
and I try to explain to her that I wasn't actually asking the questions,
but wanted to know if they thought it was creepy

LET'S GO FOR A WALK

because I think it's creepy
and I don't think she believes me
so I finish my beer, shake John's hand, say goodbye to Billy,
and exit the bar.

I consider a third round,
but realize the world now looks like a dream,
and not in a Shakespearean sort of way.
I head back to my apartment, open the door,
hear a garbled-cat-like-wail,
and assume I must have stepped on his tail.
I feel bad, but at the same time
feel a bit of justice for him chewing on my cord.

I throw up a couple of times (in the toilet...no muss, no fuss),
sit down, and wait for my roommates to come home.
They give me some Alka-Seltzer and promptly send me to bed.

And so I finish this,
a night full of choices that don't amount to anything
but some pen on paper
and smudged ink on the side of my hand.

LET'S GO FOR A WALK

2014

LET'S GO FOR A WALK

We Five's "You were on my mind"
(01/13/2014)

Walking around with a song in my head...

"...When I woke up this morning,
you were on my mind
and you were on my mind..."

and I can't stop thinking of her.
She who's the reason I smoke
and when you look into my eyes and see,
y'know that sad spot
the one where you feel that certain spur of sympathy
for me
and you don't know why
well that's where she lives
and no matter how much time
has gone by
since I've spoken to her,
or spoken of her...

and I can't shake her out of me.

And it gets harder
when other things in my life
aren't going so well.
When I fear that everything
that got me here,
to this city,
might slip away at any moment
when I feel ostracized and isolated

and I feel the type of loneliness that only she could relate to.

"....I got troubles
whoa whoaah
I got worries
whoa whoaaah
I got wounds to bind..."

This world that's consistently
trying to change me,
make me tough,
make me mean
and I fucking refuse to be.
My stubbornness
to not lose myself.
To not lose
what makes me, me.
To not lose that empathy,
to not lose this fucking urge
to express myself
and speak at every interval
of heightened emotion.

I won't self-censor my eyes.
I won't stop seeing the beauty
around me,
no matter how many times
it tells me to look away.

And she,
the only other crusader
I've met so far.
She who was the most beautiful

LET'S GO FOR A WALK

she who was the biggest rejection.

"...So I went to the corner,
just to ease my pain
yeah, just to ease my pain
I got troubled
whoa whoaah
I got worried
whoa whoaah
I came home again..."

And so I turn each corner,
not knowing what lays ahead
but not expecting anything good.
Not wanting anything good
still not wanting a thing besides her.
Knowing that if she called me tonight,
if she told me that she changed her mind
and loved me back
that I would leave this place.
I would leave my job.
I would leave any future behind,
just to live in the past with her.

And FUCK what do I do!?
I've given up
and I mean that in the current-past tense.
I gave up a long time ago
and I haven't had any sense
of hope
any idea at all

on how to attain happiness
and completion
without her presence
without her support
without her.

"...I got troubles
whoa whoaah
I got worries
whoa whoaah
I got wounds to bind..."

So
I go home,
I entertain myself,
I get up,
I go to work,
I go home,
I distract myself,
I get up,
I go to work,
I come home,
I'm starting to not recognize myself.

I don't know what I want anymore.
I come here,
and I talk a lot of shit,
and I feel catharsis
but I no longer know what good it does me.
What can it do to speak of
the beginning and middle,
when I have no idea how it ends

LET'S GO FOR A WALK

how it resolves
or if it does at all.

"...Yeah I got a feeling
down in my shoes
yeah way down in my shoes..."

I'm speaking to a mirror.
I speak to others who have felt
my kind of, or some sort of,
pain.
The kind of pain that becomes you,
the type of pain that can conquer you
completely
if you don't let it go.

"...yeah I gotta ramble whoa whoaah,
I gotta move on whoa whoaah,
I gotta walk away my blues..."

"...So I woke up this morning,
you were on my mind..."

Of course
you were on my mind.

LET'S GO FOR A WALK
03/23/2014

I feel terrified and anxious.
The world is a blurry canvas.
The paint drifting off onto the wall.

Can't decide what's real and what's not.
All I know is that she has been missing.
I told her to go and she left,
and she's missing in my heart.
I'm not full anymore.
I can't understand how to feel content.
I try man I fucking try,
I've been pretending
but pretending does not keep you warm at night.

So I crack open my window
when it's 30 degrees outside
because I need to remind myself
that outside exists.
And I fear so much
that no one understands.
Maybe I really am the only one here
that experiences these things.
Even though people say that they relate
no one else is in my head but me.

And I think that's it
she used to be
in my head with me.
I wasn't alone in here
although I had her mind though,

her body always belonged to others.
And the jealousy I felt was insufferable.
Now the loneliness I feel is inconsolable.

And there aren't words.
These sounds don't explain
the feeling of my guts,
in the center of my chest,
twisting and tightening when I see her eyes
in my head
her hair
in my head
her voice
in my head
her touch
in my head
her name
ringing in the back of my ears.

And the years
have gone by
in the blink of an eye.
Her soul
wanders off
missing me.
And I can remember
lying on the floor
looking at the ceiling,
us next to each other,
minds kissing.
I can remember
with perfect clarity

LET'S GO FOR A WALK

driving on a hot summer day,
windows down,
she takes my cigarette,
tosses it out the window,
smiles at me,
and I'm not angry,
just happy that she smiled.

Because if she wanted me to stop, then I'd stop.

But she couldn't love me
like I needed her to.
And I couldn't not love her
like she needed me to.
And so I had to tell her to go
and so she left.

The following poem's title comes from, at the time, the open mic I was attending allowed six minutes for every poet.

Six Minute Me
(05/31/2014)

I keep listening to my thoughts.
My inactions that are substitutes for actualizations.
I am so dishonest, with my ineptitude
to rely on words to describe things.
People believe that I am good at it.
But the truth is,
I'm such a good liar
I've just convinced them that is so.
In truth,
I can not describe anything.
I can only describe myself.
And I'm so fucking sick of myself.
But obviously I'm not
or I wouldn't be writing about me all the time.
The truth is
that I only feel safe
about myself.
I only feel like I could understand
about myself.
The only thing I could be
is by myself.
The idea of letting someone else
into my heart,
into my thoughts...
the idea of putting myself into another,
being enveloped,

being with...
the idea of it scares the living shit out of me.

The laws of physics
are based on causality.
All the universe
works in causes and effects.
However, I do not.
I feel like an exception to the rule
because my effects have no causes
and causes without effect
and to believe in cause and effect is to assume Time exists
and to believe in Time assumes linearity
and to believe in linearity,
then there must be a form of fatalism or destiny
and to believe in all of that
means that every action we take matters...effects...is important
and to believe that is too much fucking responsibility for me to handle
so I shut down
I break reality,
I convince myself that 'life is but a dream'
and that someday I'll wake up
in a mental institution somewhere
and be told that I've been hallucinating my successes,
that it really did all fall apart,
that I don't have any real freedom.

So, I need to just be.
I need to be,
in order to embrace reality.
I can't go on trying to be 'something'
no matter that that 'something'

LET'S GO FOR A WALK

is dynamic and changes from situation to situation.
I can't be something.
I can't be someone.
I need to be.

I mean you all feel it too right?
The pressure to be someone right now
or something...right?
So, let's just not do it right now.
I'm telling you right now,
I'm scared writing this.
I don't want to do it.
And, I feel silly addressing a crowd of people
that doesn't yet exist.
And it fucks with my whole 'destiny' thing even more
to know that,
in a couple of days
you will all exist
as a crowd
in the future 'this' room.
And I'll be telling you all of my feelings
and I'll then no longer be afraid to write this,
but be terrified to read this
as I always am.
But this time
I'm not going to pretend at all.
I'm going to say to you,
"I'm fucking scared right now
and I don't want to read this to you
and I didn't want to write this.
But I did anyway,

LET'S GO FOR A WALK

because I need catharsis
and I did anyway,
because I think some of you might feel the same as I do
and so if you're scared right now
fuck it
be scared
and if you're hungry right now,
don't wait for me to finish reading
grab something to eat
and if you're horny right now
then check out whoever you are attracted to
and don't feel ashamed
Just be right now."
And then I'll walk off the stage
and I'll sit back down
and I'll start pretending again.
I'll put on whatever demeanor
is appropriate to the situation
and so will you.

And so how do I function
in a world
where I can't just be and feel and FUCK it makes me so FUCKING ANGRY,
sometimes I want to scream
sometimes I'm honestly jealous
of the homeless people in this city
that are just screaming nonsense at people,
because I want to do that.
I want to just talk nonsense.
I want to fucking tear my clothes off and start dancing and singing
on the subway.
FUCK!

LET'S GO FOR A WALK

And I forget sometimes
sometimes I forget,
like right now,
why I do it.
Why do I care to be
in this society
at all.
I don't understand it.
I don't ever feel fully accepted
and I mean,
that I've never felt
like I fully 100% *fit*
anywhere
and I don't think I ever will
and I don't know even if I'm supposed to.

My grandfather used to tell me
that I was born too soon.
He believed that in a thousand years,
other people will be like me.
That I was non-competitive
that I was honest
that I was exceptionally sympathetic and empathetic to everyone,
even those I didn't like.
And I feel strange about this.
I mean
I'm happy because he loved me
and I loved him.
But I'm sad,
because all of the things that he mentioned
means that I have a responsibility
to be

LET'S GO FOR A WALK

to continue to exist
to pass those traits on.
And I don't want to
because the only times I can open up
is for six minutes in front of a crowd,
once a week.
We don't live in a world
where it's easy for me
to be me
beyond that.
But maybe it's a start.
Six minutes of me a week.
Where no one can tell me to shut up
no one can interrupt me
six minutes,
and I probably won't even use them all.

Not Angry Poem
(06/18/2014)

The heat is overwhelming me.
Can't think
because of the insanity
brought on
by depriving oxygen
and sweltering humidity.
Fans do no justice
when the air feels like a hot tub.

And I wrote a poem
an incredibly angry poem.
I do not like this poem.
I'd rather write a poem
about a poem I've written
that I didn't like,
than read the poem
I didn't like
to a crowd of people
that are just as angry
and frustrated as I am
on a hot summer day.

I tried to write
about how I am a man,
and there are women
that are angry at men,
and I had my heart broken
by a woman,
so I am not a bad man.

LET'S GO FOR A WALK

However,
the poem I wrote
makes me look like a bad man
because it seemed like I was angry at women,
when really
I am angry at one woman
the one who broke my heart
which is exactly the point
I was trying to make about women
who are angry at men
perhaps the men
who broke more than their hearts though.

And to go into more detail
would have me recite the poem itself
so let's stop this train of thought
here.

Which makes me think to hyperlink
"here"
because I am a web developer,
and "here"
always links to somewhere,
and somewhere
would be there
so here and there
are always the same
especially
since you reach both destinations
while sitting in front of your computer.
Which leads me to wonder
is a virtual destination

LET'S GO FOR A WALK

the same thing
as an actual destination.

And what is the problem with this wireless router
going in and out of contact with my computer.
Perhaps it was a sign
to not email that poem
before I had some time
to think
to not send this to my phone
before I had a chance to reconsider.
Time Warner,
this is the first good service
you have performed for me.
Thank you.

And I've been thinking
about men and women
a lot lately.
Been thinking about how,
on the subway
I overheard a mother
tell her young daughter
to close her legs.
How strange no father
tells his son
to do the same.

And while browsing my facebook
I read my friends posts
about "rape culture"
and "yes all women".

LET'S GO FOR A WALK

When I realize
the difference between
myself and other men
that I've encountered.
We all appreciate
the beauty of women
and yes,
I think I mean "all"
men, women, straight, gay,
all genders, all sexes
can appreciate feminine beauty.
But there is the type of person
that when he sees beauty
wishes to own it
to conquer.
However,
when I see beauty
a sunset, stars, art, women
I do not wish to possess,
but feel overwhelmed
and full just by viewing.
And in many cases
the desire to subdue,
can remove the light
that made something so beautiful
to begin with.
Instead to coexist,
is to uplift
and make mutual appreciation.

But how I wish
for some precipitation,

LET'S GO FOR A WALK

to calm my nerves
and put a damp rag
on my everlasting mourning of
love lost or
never found or
imagined or
yet to be.

And so I sit here
typing on a hot laptop.
I sit here
with my cat next to me
sprawled out on the floor
telling me she requires belly rubs
immediately.
And so I show her some love,
put some ice cubes in her water bowl,
and promise that tonight will be cooler
and acknowledge
that hot summer days
are no time for
angry poetry.
And acknowledge
that tonight will be better
after a cold beer
and good company.

LET'S GO FOR A WALK
07/28/2014

Tonight I have to drink to write.
Or rather I drink so I will write.
Or rather drinking makes me forget that I am writing.

Again the thoughts swivel and swerve.
The idea I had weeks ago
is a treble in the symphony
of boisterous mumblings.
"The idea"
makes me sound so profound,
when I do not think of myself as such.
My grandfather was profound
the most intelligent man I will ever know
and I will speak of him over and over.
But people have mistaken his insights for my own.
How silly.
How ridiculous.
I am not intelligent
just because I know intelligent people.
I am not wise
just because I have accepted, and passed on, wisdom.

I think I think of myself as an idiot.
I think I am a fool.
I think I do things that seem obviously mistaken.
I think therefore I think.
I think that thinking is the most overrated thing there is.
I think that thinking is a non-action.
I think that life is about actions,
and thinking is about imagination.

LET'S GO FOR A WALK

I think therefore I live in a dream.

I imagine myself in other places
while standing on a subway.
In my fantasy I have finally lost it
given up all hope of sanity and am inconsolable.
I mean, no one can get me out of my bed
not my best friend / roommate
not my sister or her adorable beagle Lola.
But then my family and friends finally realize to call you
and you come
and I start crying and grab you
and keep telling you that I'm sorry that I couldn't get over you
and you lye next to me and tell me it doesn't matter now
and you get me to eat and drink
and I tell you that I am afraid to get out of bed
and go back to the sane world
because it will mean that you will leave again
and you tell me that you will never leave me
and we lye together
and I get it all out...I mean all of it
and I'm free
and with you
and happy.

Then a pretty girl stands in front of me
and I'm pushed to the back of the train
with her hair in my face
as she converses with a friend of hers
completely ignoring my body and mind behind her
and I think what a perfect analogy for you
and I think about the lyrics to the songs

LET'S GO FOR A WALK

playing through my headphones
and I think that some music
can be a suitable substitute for sex, hunger, and even love
and I think one of those songs is Maps by the Yeah Yeah Yeahs
and I think this is my stop so I get off.

I get off and I get on,
and it's always a struggle always a terrible game
of whether I will kill myself before I accomplish everything I need to.
And I don't even remember what that was anymore.
I remember for the longest time I thought my life was *about* something.
That there was a need for me
that there was something I was supposed to do.
But without you
I don't even remember.
I don't know what my purpose was,
and I don't know how to live without one.

Was it something about understanding?
Wasn't I supposed to seek knowledge?
Wasn't I so insatiably hungry
for different perspectives
and to understand the world around me
so I could help it
so I could create change for the better?
But why?
It seems so stupid now.
It seems so ignorant that I could do anything like that.
Listen, I know that one man can make a difference.
But I am *not* that man.
I will not leave my mark on this world
and I no longer believe that is my path

LET'S GO FOR A WALK

and I think my path leads to a cliff
and I think that cliff leads to a bottomless pit of echos
and I think somewhere at the bottom is a memory of you
and I think that's why I want to go there.

I take another sip of my Blue Moon Beer
the beer I got from the Rite Aid on the corner
and I whisper in my own ear to,
"Let it go man...just let it go. Let it slither on through..."

But it's just too much.
I don't know how to ease my pain.
And this sucks
I want to erase this.
This is not poetry
or philosophy
or even so much as a rant.
It's complaining!
Endless complaining
that I loved someone
that didn't love me back!
So fucking what?
Nobody cares to hear that.
Write something meaningful if you're going to write.
Write something uplifting.
Write something that will make things better
don't write this
don't write about the sadness
it's useless
it turns lights off and closes doors
it sheds tears and makes people pity you
it's not ethical

LET'S GO FOR A WALK

it's not moral
it's egocentric and lurid.
It's vividly masturbatorial.
But here I am telling you all of this
here I am because I feel the need
to vomit up my confusion once more.

Another sip, another beer.

Another wish to wash away my fear.

Another sip on the tip of my tongue.

Another wish you were the one.

Another languid flaccid lie,

that I could ever say goodbye.

How foolish sounding a poem

that I actually attempted to rhyme.

Wow man I can't even criticize myself properly.
I have introduced a notion that is not fulfilled here.
Don't listen to a god damned thing I say
because I have more pride than I am telling you.
I am too proud to get over her.
I am too proud to deal with the reality that I am just another guy.
I am even too proud to really convince you I am proud.
The truth is that I can still have a purpose if I want one.
The truth is that I don't anymore
and I don't know why so I blame lost love.
The truth is that she was but a dream and I was but a dreamer.

LET'S GO FOR A WALK

The truth is that I don't know where to go from here.
The truth is that I would rather think than do,
and I would rather dream than wake,
and I would rather feel pain than true happiness,
and I would rather stop now before I embarrass myself anymore.
But I don't want to leave this completely hopeless.
I don't want to leave you with my sadness in your heart.
I don't ever want to stop talking.
I don't ever want to stop writing.
But to do so would mean more thinking
and that is something that needs to stop.

I Think I'll Still Get Drunk
(09/26/2014)

I recall being in college
and having the thought,
"If I drink,
something will happen.
I'm bored
and if I *drink*
something will *definitely* happen."
I got drunk
and then I was just bored and drunk.

Well now I use that logic for writing.
But half the time it actually works.
And half the time I'm just drunk yelling at my laptop.

So FUCK YOU!
Yeah that's right
I said FUCK YOU,
and I know it's cliche
to be an angry FUCKIN' writer
but fuck everything and everyone and their mothers and fathers
and sisters and brothers
fuck your cousins and aunts
and uncles and nephews
and nieces and grandparents.

I think this stress is induced
because it's been three years now
since I've spoken to her.
And my heart is gone.

LET'S GO FOR A WALK

It's just fucking gone.
And fuck I'm sad about it.
I mean look at me.
I gained 20 pounds since then.
I haven't really dated since then.
I haven't even really been interested
in anyone else since then.
And I keep writing about her
because she's on my mind.
I keep writing about her
because she's the most significant
and beautiful thing
I've ever had in my life.
And "my life"
doesn't seem like the right phrase here...

Sometimes I smoke cigarettes
just to smell the smoke on my fingers.
That smoke smells like High School.
That smoke smells like feelings
of lust and complete hopelessness.
That smoke reminds me
that there is a part of me
that's completely suicidal
and welcomes the cancer fates.

And here I am
writing about smoking again.
So here's another one
that I could never actually put in print
for fear that my mother would read it
and have a panic attack that her son is a smoker

that none of the 5 billion talks we had
about smoking mattered
that none of it mattered
since I have anxiety
and god damn it's the only thing that'll clear my head
for a second a minute actually maybe 5.

And I'm being told now that people identify with me.
That there are those that love my thoughts,
my voice,
that I need to keep writing.
But it's not a choice.
I have to write.
I have no say in the matter.
My fingers get antsy
and I'd completely erupt
and go into hysteria
if I no longer had my hands and / or my voice.
I need to express myself in words.
It's just what seems to happen,
the alcohol just hurries it along.

I was going to say that,
"I really don't want to have her on my mind,"
but of course I do.
I just want to be on hers.
In that way.

And yes,
I know she thinks about me.
And yes,
I know that she misses me.

LET'S GO FOR A WALK

I know that
because every couple of months
she messages me
and lets me know that.

And I don't know what's right here.
I don't know if I'm supposed to resist her.
I don't know if I was supposed to give up on her.

It seemed rational.

It seemed justified.

It seemed like the only way to move on.

But I haven't moved on.

It's very confusing.

And I don't know what more I need to do.
I don't know if there's a way to feel good about myself.
I don't know how to satiate
my feelings of starvation and longing
for the emotional mental sexual attraction connection
that I had with that tiny blue eyed blonde haired hippy
pot head artist photographer
with the voice of an angel I dreamt of when I was a kid.

All I got is words
I want music,
I want to play,
I want to sing,
but all I got is words.

LET'S GO FOR A WALK

I want to paint
I want to draw,
but all I got is words.

I want to climb
I want to compete,
but all I got is words.

I want money,
but all I got is words.

I want women,
but all I got is words.

All I got is words
so I give the only thing I got away
and dance around the fact
that it's the in-betweens the spaces the white parts
the silence that's really where the meaning lies
the part where you stop hearing or reading me
the part where the synapse fires and triggers
the same part of your brain that's poisoning mine.

And so in my fit of writing rage
a friend yells my name outside my window,
my mother texts me that she loves me,
my sister calls me,
and my cat jumps on my bed
and is looking at me while purring
and so I decompress
although I think I'll still get drunk.

Unpolished
(10/18/2014)

I've been getting a bit annoyed
when people have been suggesting
that I get out of my "comfort zone".
I've been diagnosed with General Anxiety Disorder
which makes it sound like,
"oh well that's just the run of the mill 'General' version."
When actually it means
that I have anxiety
over pretty much everything.
My point is
that I don't have a "comfort zone".
I am scared of things that I do everyday.
I am scared to go outside some days.
I am scared to even get out of bed some days,
because I'll have to do things
figure out a way to make the most of the day / my life.
I'll have to talk to people.
I'll have to try to be clear to not be misunderstood.
I'm *terrified* of being misunderstood!
That might even be the reason
why people say that I'm so well spoken / a good writer.
I think it's because
I have an insatiable desire
to be clear
because if someone goes around
telling people that I said something...
something that I didn't mean to say...
then people might get the wrong idea about who I am

LET'S GO FOR A WALK

and have false expectations of me
or think of me negatively for unjust cause
or even like me for someone that they *think* I am.

I know I'm not the only one
that experiences life this way either.
I have met a good amount of people
who have the same anxieties that I do,
and go through the same shit.
But they all seem to be people
that I can't seem to keep in touch with
probably because we share these anxieties in common
such as hating talking on the phone,
or making plans,
or writing emails.

And so it always leads to me feeling alone.

And you know what's absolutely crazy?
With having all this anxiety,
for pretty much my entire life,
I was never afraid of death...
not really anyway...
not as a real thing...
until this freaken year.
For some reason I can't stop thinking about it now.
I mean, one inevitable day
I am going to die
and there's nothing I can do about it.
My consciousness will seize to exist.
Everything will stop.
I mean there is the chance that there's an after-life.

LET'S GO FOR A WALK

I mean maybe my consciousness won't stop
maybe it'll continue somehow
but there is no scientific proof of that.
There's scientific proof
that the components that make up who I am,
will be dispersed into other things
but my consciousness (the thing made from these components),
I think is different...
I think is what spiritual people would call the soul...
I think it's what makes me unique...
and I think that stops...that ends.
But maybe I'm wrong.
In fact I really hope that I am
because I really don't want to end...ever.
I know that's crazy.
I know it's strange too,
especially since I just detailed
how my life isn't all very happy
and relaxing all the time.
But I just don't want to end.
It's not even about being remembered and living on through others.
I've realized that I want to be the one remembering forever.
I don't know, maybe this is a good thing
maybe I've been depressed
and to get out of that
the first step is realizing that I want to live.
But right now I mostly feel terror about it.

Which I think is leading to prophetic dreams...
dreams / hopes that I am more than just a simple mortal human...
dreams that make me feel like that I am a hero
or I am special somehow

LET'S GO FOR A WALK

or that I have superhuman abilities.

The other night
I had a dream
that I was walking down a street at night.
A woman was walking towards me.
She was very attractive
and had long red hair.
As she approached she said,
"Hello, Jonathan Cherlin."
She knew my full name,
although I had never met her before.
She said her name was Alex
and she told me things about myself
that I had never told anyone…
things that only I could know…
things that my waking self has now forgotten.
She then told me,
"In four days, you will make a decision that will effect the rest of your life."

Four days later
was this past Tuesday.
I had been sick since the day before,
but decided to go into work anyway
since I felt a bit better.
The entire day
I thought that something might happen
that a situation might arise that'd effect the rest of my life.
Even so, I realized that all choices
whether they seem big or small
could end up having a larger impact on our lives
than we realize at the time.

LET'S GO FOR A WALK

As I continued my day,
I felt more sick.
Finally, in the evening,
I arrived at home
feeling exhausted.
I had been excited though,
since I was supposed to receive in the mail
a new video game I had been looking forward to.
I had even spent $15 extra
to have it delivered to me on the first day of release
since I often work late,
and don't usually have time to go to the video game stores
before they close.
However, I got a slip saying
that it needed to be signed for
and that they'd try again tomorrow.
This sort of pissed me off.
I called the number on the back of the slip
and asked if there was any chance
that I could pick it up tonight...they said yes.
So I got the address,
and went on a half-hour trek
to Hunters Point Ave.
to find a UPS warehouse
and pick up my package.
As I got off at the Hunters Point Ave. station
I felt feverish walking down a barren street
with tall buildings at night in a fairly dark area.
It felt very much like a dream.
I found the warehouse,
and as I waited I couldn't shake the feeling

LET'S GO FOR A WALK

that I had been there before
but I have no idea why
in any situation I would have.
But it just felt so familiar.
A lot of the UPS workers
were checking out for the night
and joking around with the security guard.
It made me feel comfortable,
almost like being at home.
My father was very much a handy man,
and was always very comfortable
around blue collar workers,
although wouldn't be considered one himself.

I received my package
and made my way back home.
I spent some time trying out my new game,
until I couldn't keep my eyes open anymore.
The next morning I awoke with a fever
and could barely function,
having to completely miss a day of work.
So, I don't know if this day will effect the rest of my life…
all I can see is that it made me more sick and confused.

And none of this seems satisfying.
I just wish that I felt more than fear and sadness.
I want to feel calm but can't.
I want to feel love, but can't really
because I associate that with fear now too.
And knowing all of this,
and knowing I'm going to die…
it all seems so melodramatic, amateurish, teenage-angst-like…

LET'S GO FOR A WALK

and I am far now from those teenage days.

But life is murky.
I don't quite know what I want or where I'm going
or how not to feel scared.
So when you say to me,
"...maybe you should get out of your comfort zone..."
just know that I'll laugh a little inside
and maybe cry a little too
'cause I really don't know what you mean.

LET'S GO FOR A WALK

10/26/2014

Causality is
if, then
then
if, then
then
if, then...
causality is infinite.
Does it go in one direction?
I don't think it does,
but I can't explain it with causal logic.
But then causality
has led to me thinking
these thoughts
which leads me to believe
that every thought
must have some sort of logic behind it.
Of course I remember
learning about the difference
between validity and soundness.
That a sound argument
requires it to be true.
But of course
this leads to the most singular question
of what is "Truth",
or even does objective "Truth" exist?

I wonder about Time.
I wonder about Time constantly.
I wonder if Time exists
because I very often feel out of it

both in the sense that I've used it up,
and in the sense that I'm out of place.
Again leading back to the feeling
that I'm not here...
that this is all a dream or an illusion.
That any answer given to me
is a product of my own mind,
so how can I really learn any new information
if I can only understand according to my interpretations?

This is where I imagine imagination comes in.
I must picture myself as someone else...
something else...
somewhere else.
Which in turn
feels like a dream within a dream.
It's my mind
pretending to be my mind
as if I were another product of my mind.

I've been told by people that I am brilliant...
highly intelligent.
I've even been told,
from time to time,
that I'm a genius.
But I think
I'm just a highly articulate confused person...
a very confused person
that's able to articulate in a moderately accurate way
how confused I really am.

LET'S GO FOR A WALK

I don't know how many people
question their respective realities.
I don't know, myself,
how to happily live with that.
I wouldn't encourage it.
But for some reason
it's something I've done
as far back as I can remember.

LET'S GO FOR A WALK

11/15/2014

Disillusion...
I remember the first time I heard that word.
I was in my sophomore year of college
and I was sitting on Pia's bed
she was a friend
a good friend
we were intimate.
I'm pretty sure she wanted to fuck me,
and I sort of wanted to fuck her too
but just not enough to actually go through with it
because I needed a friend
a good friend.
I don't remember what she was saying
she was disillusioned about,
but I remember her saying the word,
and I remember I looked it up later,
and I remember thinking that I had felt that
about most things in life already.

It's funny
because that must have been about
10 years ago
or more than that now.
It's funny
because my mind does not comprehend
the passing of a decade
since I sat on Pia's dorm room bed.
It's funny

LET'S GO FOR A WALK

because I haven't spoken to her
in nearly that long,
and when I think about her
it's mostly filled with
a longing for the comfort
she gave me at that time
her being my friend
although when drunk,
lying on top of me
convincing me to feel her tits
on that same bed I heard the word.

And I find that discrepancy
between different kinds of intimacy
to be a common theme in my life.
That physical and emotional
never match up.
I've loved girls I never kissed,
and I've fucked girls I never loved.
This is frustrating.
I feel an intense hunger,
the kind that comes with heartbreak,
the kind that comes with rejection,
the kind that comes
when body and heart
can not catch up to each other
one seems to always be ahead of the other.

So sometimes I take long showers,
thinking of the girls
from my past
that wanted to fuck me

LET'S GO FOR A WALK

and that I wanted to fuck
and none of it is satisfying
and I go to bed bewildered
by the amount of time
I've wasted, in rooms,
thinking about girls.
And again I'll speak a bit
about how thinking is my ultimate enemy
how thinking is the most inactive
how thinking is the me that I'd like to shut up
that if I acted more without thinking,
I might have some better stories to tell
although I might not have the know how to tell them.

And I've realized there's a cadence to my thoughts
a slow cadence reminiscent of the blues.
And when I hear that guitar play,
it reminds me of my father,
it reminds me of the lullabies he'd strum me to sleep with,
it reminds me that the hunger is in my blood my DNA.

So is this about her?
I can't remember anymore...
is this about Rachel?

Every poem I write
is somehow about Rachel.
All of them.
Every thought I have
is somehow about Rachel.
Everything I see
somehow relative to her...

LET'S GO FOR A WALK

everything...
to the point that I wonder
if it really is.
If I can really want someone that much
if I really ever felt *that* connected to her
that maybe I made it up.
That maybe I made *her* up.
That maybe I never kissed her,
not because I was afraid to lose her,
but maybe I was afraid to lose the idea of her
I had made.

It's difficult to come to terms with these things.
It's difficult to admit that my only nemesis is me
that I'm the one holding myself back from happiness
and I don't know why and, more importantly,
I don't know how to stop it in any honest way
in a way that doesn't feel like a lie.

And I honestly just want to get drunk right now.
I want to go out, buy a bottle of wine, and drink up.
And I want to think that's the only way I can write this but
the truth is my writing is much better when I'm sober
the truth is that the fear of expression
makes the sweetest sounding sorrow.

And I wonder if I'll ever learn how to play that riff in my head.
And I wonder if I'll ever find a way to draw that picture
in the back of my eyes.
And I wonder if every blonde I see
will stop reminding me of Rachel.
And I wonder if it'll ever feel okay to say her name.

LET'S GO FOR A WALK

And I wonder if I'll ever write something that satisfies me.
And I wonder if people will remember my name.
And I wonder if I'll ever fulfill my dream
of people remembering my actions instead...
if I'll create something that lives on...
if people will look for who created it...
the true immortality...
the true creation...
to create something remembered,
and to be forgotten.

But mostly I think I'll be disillusioned.
That my fantasies will never match my realities.
That disappointment will reign,
since I never live up to what I think I can...
that all the praise I'll ever receive
will pale in comparison to what I wished to accomplish.

LET'S GO FOR A WALK

12/09/2014

When I was younger
it seemed like everyone else
had the answers...
everyone seemed so confident around me...
everyone seemed to be telling me how I was supposed to act, be, think.
But the older I get
the more I realize that they're all full of shit...
that they are so confident,
not because they have the answers,
but because they've never thought
to ask the proper fucking questions.

I'm realizing my confidence now.
I am realizing also how completely jaded I sound
but I don't think I am.
I don't see these things in black and white / positive and negative.
I don't see anything in polar extremes.
I don't believe anything is completely anything.
Everything is mixed and full and destroyed all at the same time.
I see the beginning and the end of things
in a flash a flutter of my eye
and I don't know how to verbalize it
and *that's* the reason it doesn't make sense
but it doesn't not make it so.

Stream of consciousness
is designed to have revelations.
It's funny
because people don't think
that true stream of consciousness

can be considered as "designed"
because there's not supposed to be a plan.
But there's not really a plan for anything in life
but there is infinite foresight.

Chemical reactions are predictable
we know
that two oxygens
and one hydrogen
make water
every time...
and if we don't know it,
then we don't know
that we don't know it...
we don't know when we're wrong
until the exact moment we do.

So according to what we know,
everything in the Universe
is predictable
since everything
is essentially chemical reactions.
Therefore,
how I will end this
is already written in a way.
It's been decided already
and I'm just playing through it
like an actor in a play.
I've known this all
a very long time
and it contributes
to my feeling of detachment

because maybe FUCK IT maybe I'm fucking perceiving the world
in a larger fucking way than most people do.

Or,
it's all convoluted paranoia.
I've made it all up
and it's just a way to not engage,
to not truly feel happy,
to see the end before I get there
and to not fully appreciate
and take the risks necessary
to fully enjoy the journey.

Can it be both?
Can both be true somehow?
I don't know.
I feel like though
that when I read this,
this will be about the point
that I lose the attention of my audience
or at least some of them…
some of you.

It's because those pauses…
those spaces between each word…
in my brain they are *not* silent…
in fact that is where
the bulk of my thoughts exist.
It's just they don't make sense enough
by the time they form
some portion of a word
but if you knew what those spaces meant

LET'S GO FOR A WALK

it might make sense to you
and I might not feel so alone.

And it does make me angry
that no matter how much I speak
I feel like I am not saying anything.
I feel the hunger of knowing
that each word
is a mistranslation
each syllable
hitting the wrong tone
each sentence
giving the illusion
that I've expressed a thought
when I've really
just written something
that doesn't have any resemblance to thought
since thought has no visual equal.

And music sometimes gives me respite
but even music has it's limits
even music must sound like something.

I found a person that read my spaces,
and I fell in love with her,
and I miss her always,
but she did not love me back
and it hurt so I wrote her off
and now there's too many signals
and I still feel her
and I want to respond but can't and…
too many signals from her brain to mine…

LET'S GO FOR A WALK

too much want from her to talk to me...
but maybe I'm just crazy...
maybe I am...
maybe that's impossible...
maybe I'm not...
maybe I just need to see her...
maybe that'd make everything better...
or maybe it would be the final thing to make me stop.

And it all seems like a bunch of maybes.

That's what it is. All life is just a bunch of maybes.

And I live in a world that I am possible.

LET'S GO FOR A WALK
12/16/2014

This is about something deeper than a text message.
It is more complicated than a simple reply.
This is about my relationship with women in general now.
Not just you.
This is about every girl that's stood me up.
It's about every girl that raved about how wonderful I was,
but not enough to date me.
And I know it's cliche to be who I am and want what I want.
And I know it's cliche to talk about unrequited love.
And I know it's cliche to talk about being the "nice guy".
And I know all these things,
and I know if I reply to you
then it makes everything okay.
It makes it okay for you to walk all over me,
to manipulate me,
to use me in the most unflattering of ways.
And by "you",
I mean all you girls out there that would do the same...
that I'm tired,
actually fucking exhausted
making it alright for you to manipulate me
emotionally like this.
And god damn if some of you make this about sex
I swear to god I'll scream!
I'm not mad because I'm not getting laid...
in fact if I just wanted to get laid
then I most likely wouldn't even have this problem.
I just want companionship.
I want to go for a fucking walk and grab a cup of coffee...

LET'S GO FOR A WALK

you know spend some time with someone.
If it evolved into romance then fine,
but if I am going out with you
it means that there's something about you
that I like that is more than physical…
male or female or other.

The real question is do I even want to reply.

The real question is,
am I just really wanting to hold on to you
just like you are holding on to me…
And by "you" I mean Ellie…
Because if I acknowledge you,
that means we get to continue
some sort of connection.
But if I don't,
then that's not guaranteed anymore.
Even though we never really had any grand connection in the first place.
But I liked you.
And I liked spending time with you…
you know that whole coffee thing.
And fucking I loved your brain.
But after so many times of you cancelling on me
an hour before we planned to go out…
Well that's just not okay with me anymore.

And so you text me a reminder of something I said three years ago.
Something I said that was funny and wise…
something you said that you found on your "timehop app"…
something you said you "love".
And I sit here staring at the screen

LET'S GO FOR A WALK

because it's been only three days ago
since you left me to drink alone another night away.

But in the end I'll succumb.
In the end I'll respond,
"Ha! Sounds like something I'd say."

And then I'll put down the phone.
And I'll feel like shit all over again.

LET'S GO FOR A WALK

2015

LET'S GO FOR A WALK
01/31/2015

I recently went back
and looked through
all my writings from the past three years.
And they all share
the same themes
on a systematic loop
from Hell.
I'm stuck in a rut.
I write about honesty,
and I write about Rachel,
and I write about loneliness,
and those are just the things that I write about.
No new experiences,
no real connection with the world outside my body.
This distance is debilitating
and it hurts to see the world in front me
but be incapable of embracing its' reality.
I've felt every relationship I've had with anyone
fade into a dream...
and the dreams even fade into a darkness
that I've only sort of heard about in ghost stories.
I feel this icicle that's started from the center of me
slowly drip droplets into my circulatory system
each beat of my heart gets colder
and I freeze up.

Honesty:

I don't know how to do it anymore.
Everything I say sounds like bullshit...

LET'S GO FOR A WALK

and yes, even fucking that.
I can't fucking explain how I feel anymore
because it's empty...
it's filled with void and blackness...
which is y'know,
the absence of light...
which leads to....

Rachel:

The only person I've known
that could pull me out of myself...
because it's like if you are tired in the morning,
but it's time to get out of bed...
but instead of going out into the world,
you could just go into a much more comfortable bed...
That was my anxiety-riddled-self while conversing with Rachel.

And she contacted me again,
and I finally caved in after 3 years
and replied back with a 3 hour online conversation.
A conversation that validated everything I thought
of why she can't be with me...
but neither of us understanding it...
but just typing words to her,
while knowing she was on the other side...
well I came back to life...
for a week...
alive for a week
just from a single inaudible conversation with her...
and now I need my next fix.
And she said she's coming back to New York in a few months...

LET'S GO FOR A WALK

so let's get back on that hallucinogenic-depressive-might-cause-
heartattack-and-brain-aneurysms medicated regiment...
because, well,
I apparently have given up
any sort of hope of achieving
any sort of independence
from her kind of high.
And so....

Loneliness:

It doesn't feel good
when there's nothing left
and no one here
to hear you complain about it
anymore.
And people do reach out,
but I am thin fucking air
disappearing as soon as you breathe me in.

And so I hope to begin something again
and feel something new
and be awake.

LET'S GO FOR A WALK

04/21/2015

There's a lot of different people in this world.
And there's a lot of ways to go about things.
Some are happy, some are not.
Some desire, some are content.
Some marry, some die alone...
some are happily married, some happily alone.

But what am I? What do I want?
What is it that will make me feel content now?
And I say now,
because it's impossible to decide what will make me content later,
and what kept me content before
no longer applies here now in this moment in time.
Do you know what I mean by "Time"?
Do you know what I mean?
I mean
the transparent disillusion of self
composited to the disillusion of others
to compare what was then the self and other
to what we imagine we will be.

And I mean,
my thoughts are over my own head
so how can I expect anyone else to understand
when the words I have to describe how I feel,
at any given moment,
are at best tertiary to the emotion itself.

LET'S GO FOR A WALK

And I can talk about it til I'm blue in the face.
I could describe.
I can,
I have the capacity,
to emote.
But I only get spurts of satisfaction from it.
The true desire is to be understood.
But...
let me add to that...
I also desire to understand.

It reminds me how a month ago today,
while taking a walk at night,
I witnessed a kid hold his head out the window
of a temporarily stopped mini-van,
at 30th Ave. and 48th Street
in Astoria.
He held his face towards the sky
and repeatedly yelled,
"Dad I can see the Earth!
Dad I can see the Earth!"
I looked up.
Because for some reason that made sense to me.
That I can see the thing that I'm inside...
as a human being that makes sense.

And I mean,
I can see you looking at me.
And people love to see me looking at them.
People adore how much I can sense.
And it's exhausting.
I walk outside everyday and sense the beat,

the human organism,
the whole of any given intersection.
And feel completely separate from it,
but the pull to be a part of it.

And I'm dancing around the fact
that I've lost my mentor.
My grandfather is dead.
The man that guided these thoughts.
The man whom I always looked to make sense of the world for me...
and later to represent that sense,
or the loss of it...
He no longer exists.
I can try to think that his legacy lives on in me and others.
But the truth of the matter is
that I am no longer a student of life...
and do not feel comfortable enough to be a teacher...
that I feel like a man that comprehends but doesn't know.
Disparate and cognitively dissonant.

And I'm tired of people and their actions.
And I'm tired of having to explain.
And I'm tired of self-evaluation.
And I'm tired of the desire to write.

LET'S GO FOR A WALK
07/13/2015

Why am I trying to write something right now?
I have the slightest of conundrums.
I have lost the life of someone that I love.
I have fallen again and again
into the deepest of darkness
where comfort of blackness
dampens my lightness.
It's only now,
through the warmth of alcohol,
that some sense of language
comes into my fingertips
and allows me to click away
on letters of an old and dusty laptop.
And it's not so dusty
because of lack of use
but because of my exuberant laziness.
I try not to fall into my tropes...
you know, become a cliche of myself.
But in doing so my fingers become hesitant...angry...
they don't want to write anything at all...
they scream with desire to take control...
they don't want my brain here anymore.
So without my brain all I have is my heart and emotion...
scalding hot blood running through my eyes burning any sensation
left of comfort.
I see red and yellows,
I see the white and black of a simulation of text to paper
when numbers are fucking pretending to be words.
The thought happens that perception is reality,

LET'S GO FOR A WALK

and if I seize to perceive then nothing is real.

I laugh at the idea that people respect me.
My friend told me the other day
that confidence is when you are comfortable with yourself.
And I don't believe for a moment in my lifetime that has ever happened.
I am comfortable with a select few people,
but myself has never been one of them.

I have just come back from the gym.
My friend has been encouraging me
to work out with him 4 days a week.
I was at the gym
and needed to use a specific machine...
he doesn't have to use the machine,
but I do because I'm starting.
However, there is a pretty girl
directly next to the machine on a mat,
on the floor,
doing *strenuous* poses...
directly in front of
where I would need to be
to adjust the weights to my current threshold.
I could ask her politely to move for a moment while I do so,
but I am stunned.
I have a wash of shame, tension, anxiety, depression...
I can't talk to this girl...
I can't talk to anyone...
I want to rip my body off and rise into something else.
Tired of living, tired of trying to communicate,
I just want to be emotion and light and energy
I don't want to have to push myself anymore...

LET'S GO FOR A WALK

socially, physically, mentally.
I cower and go back to my friend.
He tells me to just tell her to move.
I see the hurt he feels when seeing my hurt.
I want to fade away, but I confront her,
she happily moves over but I can't seem to function.
My mind won't let me do what I know my body is capable of...
and I know why.
I can't lift myself on this machine,
next to the pretty girl,
because none of it is real.
And I don't know how I define reality,
but it's the only way I can explain myself.
There's no purpose to this.
I get no satisfaction from any of it.
I only feel close to the truth when I write and read,
and I can't even say why.

LET'S GO FOR A WALK
08/04/2015

I have never encountered an angry butcher.
I don't know exactly what that means,
but I have a feeling
that it has something to do with
the savage nature of mankind.
They chop up carcasses
in the back
with giant knives,
then they come up front
and speak to others
in such a calm demeanor.
Still don't know what I'm getting at.
I guess what I'm trying to say is,
I'm frustrated.
The tension of wanting someone to love,
mourning over death,
fretting over work…
Looking for answers in a void.

You know how they say that,
"You're looking for love in all the wrong places"?
What the fuck is a "wrong place"?
A place is a fucking place!
No one knows where Love is…
Where the Hell are the *right* places?

If anyone here can tell me
a sure fire way
to find love
please interrupt me

LET'S GO FOR A WALK

right now
and shout it out at the top of your lungs,
post it on facebook,
make your own website,
and never stop telling people.

And yeah...I'm that asshole
where even if you did tell me,
I wouldn't fucking believe you.
I wouldn't listen.
Because I still think it's her.

And I'm still writing about Her.

And I'm still crying about it.

And I think it's a problem.

It doesn't make sense.
There's no logic here.
There's no end where there's no logic.
And I'm sorry,
I'm sorry if I ask you how you found happiness...
because I know,
that makes you sad for me.

There's a duality.
There is reality, and fantasy...
and they're the same.

Again,
still don't know what I'm getting at.

LET'S GO FOR A WALK

And without her,
as the carrot on a stick,
I have no motivation.
I don't know why I'm walking forward.
But I know I could go for a Turkey sandwich,
and I know the butcher will smile.

LET'S GO FOR A WALK
09/26/2015

I'm coming to terms with something
that I've always known deep in my stomach,
the reason why I have knots,
the reason for all the fucking tension...
that we are living in a poor man's world.
It is the world of the impoverished,
and we are the guests on their landscape.
We do all we can to avoid the harsh reality,
that we are all just a few steps away
from sleeping on the streets that we pave.

There are more dead and poor,
than there are alive and well.
Dancing in the dark cesspool of wealth,
crying at the idea of it being taken away.
We become hostile to those who remind us
how close we are...
those that remind us that we are no different
than the man with the garbage bags on the subway.
Your fancy purse and laptop bag might hold different things...
but the differences are slighter than you think.

And this all looms over me, most days.
But today I am living in it.
Today I lost the job that would tide me over
until I found the other job that would fulfill my life,
and these are all things we say to each other and ourselves...
and we all know to a degree, that it isn't true.
We are trained to dream of jobs...

LET'S GO FOR A WALK

how fucking silly of us.

And I am more and less than my job.
I have more than a career.
I have less than a life...
or at least the life I'd rather have...
whatever that might be.

You might be smart to understand.
You might be just as brief in the breaths you have left.
But we all go to the same place when we die,
we all go back to nothingness.
No matter how much you've built on the nothingness you came from,
absence outlives presence.

This is not positive.
This is the truth in your heart, you're afraid of me to say.
Just listen for a second, and forget it.
Or run away.
Because,
this society will not change in our lifetime.
But let's at least be honest about where we stand...
on the ground,
and not in the stars.

LET'S GO FOR A WALK
09/28/2015

There's something to be said about petting an animal.
The first thing to come to terms with
is that we are the ones who are uncouth,
because I have never witnessed a person who's as graceful as a cat.
I have never witnessed a man love as purely as a dog.
Never witnessed one who listens as much as a bird.

Pet an animal and get in touch with your softer side.
Cuddle up and remember that there is something wild and playful
within you as well.
Civilization has made us most uncivilized.

I think about Rainbow and Venus...
the two cats that I grew up with.
So many stories to tell about them.
Remember,
how Venus was terrified of everything...
Remember,
how for many years I was afraid to pet her
because she would scratch me.
But in 6th grade
I read White Fang, and decided to earn her trust.
I started feeding her left-over chicken,
and gradually coercing her
to eat from my hand.
It took maybe a full month,
before she would do so.
But from that point on
we were best friends.
She would follow me around the house.

LET'S GO FOR A WALK

She would even let me pick her up from time to time.
She was an outdoor cat, which I'm told have shorter average lifespans...
but she lived to be 20-years-old.

I remember,
as she got closer to her final days,
she did not ask to go outside as often.
One day, after a long while,
she decided to come out for a bit
and rolled around the grass on our lawn.
I remember petting her and thinking
this might be the last time I see her outside
doing what she loved the most...
being wild and in nature.

A few weeks later
she had grown very weak,
and no longer seemed to be able to stand.
She mostly seemed to be sleeping,
but every now and then
would begin to move seeming confused
why she couldn't stand up.
There was still so much determination in her eyes,
so much wild,
so much.
I decided to go for a drive...rent a movie.
By the time I came back she had died.
I had been by her side all day,
but maybe she didn't want me to be there
when she passed...who knows.

LET'S GO FOR A WALK

There are similar stories about Rainbow,
who died before her,
and with other animals
that have come and gone in my life.
I'm sure at some point I will tell them.
But I believe the answer to my purpose...
the idea I'm trying to communicate...
is something I can't yet describe.

ABOUT THE AUTHOR

Jonathan Cherlin is a New York native, raised on Long Island and currently residing in Astoria. His strongest writing influences are Hideo Kojima, Kenji Eno, Walt Whitman, Robert Frost, H.G. Wells, and his Grandfather. He believes that writing is about sitting down and catching a thought.

Jonathan can often be found reading his work, and listening to others, at any given Mike Geffner Inspired Word event. He can also be seen staring at the bottom of a glass, at any given bar, across from a friend trying to make him feel better.

Jon's current profession is that of Web Developer. His life-long dream is to develop Video Games.

LET'S GO FOR A WALK

The Oded Halahmy Foundation for the arts is a 501(c) 3 non-profit cultural organization created to fund original artistic expressions of peace and hope in the Middle East, the United States and around the world.

The Foundation's projects include funding a series of prominent writers from the Middle East, many of whom have never had the opportunity to appear in print in English for the reading public. Other grants will support innovative artistic expressions of peace in poetry, drama, music, and in visual art, encouraging all forms of art as a mean of fostering the peace dialogue. Foundation events are held at the Pomegranate in SoHo, New York City

"May there peace in the Iraq, the Middle East and around the world."
– Oded Halahmy

POMEGRANATE
G A L L E R Y

137 Greene Street New York, New York, 10012
Tel: (212) 260-4014
www.poemegranategallery.com

www.ingramcontent.com/pod-product-compliance
Lightning Source LLC
Chambersburg PA
CBHW051837090426
42736CB00011B/1855